THE FINANCE DOCTOR'S
TIPS & TRICKS

JHAYNE S. SANTUCCI, JD CPA CGMA

JHAYNE S. SANTUCCI

Copyright © 2020 Jhayne S. Santucci, JD CPA CGMA

All rights reserved.

ISBN: 978-1-7359388-1-3

DEDICATION

I dedicate this to my son (R-Jay), my "Crazy" friend who
unknowingly pushed me to the path of enlightenment,
my family living in the US, Europe, Philippines,
and my "KABABAYAN" all around the world.

JHAYNE S. SANTUCCI

CONTENTS

	Acknowledgments	*vii*
	Disclaimer	*ix*
	Introduction	*xi*
1	The Uncovering	1
2	Clear Goals	pg #27
3	Basic Tax and Financial Concepts	pg #44
4	The Strategies	pg #56
5	The Gap	pg #67
6	Empowerment	pg #77
7	The Execution	pg #90
8	Life Insurance and Annuity Strategy	pg #92
9	General Securities	pg #135
10	Real Estate Law	pg #156
11	The Reward	pg #174
	Appendix	pg #192
	References	pg #199
	About the Author	pg #206

JHAYNE S. SANTUCCI

ACKNOWLEDGMENTS

Special thanks to:

The Divine, Universe, Angels, Spirit Guides, and my Higher Self for channeling the messages I had to convey in this book and for my wonderful and abundant life which I am grateful for every single day.

My Mom, who continues to inspire and motivate me even though she left us 16 years ago with breast cancer.

My family and friends have been very supportive of me.

My Editor, Melanie Barton Gauss

My Book Cover Designer, Nelma Macasinag Dakis

My Book Reviewers: Bonita Balingit, Dara Dolliole, Debbie Adkins, Jarrod Cunningham, Joe Cioffi, Johnmark Topacio Fernandez, Joseph Simmons, Kerwyn Jones, Lea Tran, Mia Thomas, Raisul Howlader, Raziel Jeremy Yamat, Renee Babcock, Riza Yamat Leak, Roy Laurens, and Victor Pazmimo Chang

JHAYNE S. SANTUCCI

DISCLAIMER

All rights reserved. No part of this book may be reproduced or transmitted, in any form, or by any means, electronic or mechanical (including photocopying), nor may it be stored in any information storage and retrieval system without written permission from the author. This content contains proprietary information. No part of this content may be used without the express written consent of the author. The advice contained in this material might not be suitable for everyone. The author designed the information to present her opinion about the subject matter. The reader must carefully investigate all aspects of any business decision before committing him or herself. The author obtained the information contained herein from sources she believes to be reliable and from her personal experience, but she neither implies nor intends any guarantee of accuracy. Should the reader need such advice, he or she must seek services from a competent professional. The author particularly disclaims any liability, loss, or risk taken by individuals who directly or indirectly act on the information contained herein. The author believes the advice presented here is sound, but readers cannot hold her responsible for either the actions they take or the result of those actions.

INTRODUCTION

How this book is written and why:

The original intent was to write a guide to simply share my life experiences and knowledge I gained, with my son, nieces, and nephews because I feel that I am the only one in the family who will be able to teach them about personal finance. The Universe had another plan. I had to expand and reach out to other young adults across the world to educate them, to expand their knowledge, to shape their thinking so that they can accomplish whatever their heart desires, despite their current condition.

Is this book for you:

- ✓ If you want to learn how to utilize Emotional Intelligence, Spiritual Knowledge, and the Financial Know-How to propel you to your wishes and dreams, then YES
- ✓ If you want to know tax/financial strategies used by the Ultra-High Net Worth Individuals to prepare you for what the Universe has for you, then YES
- ✓ If you want to know "THE REAL SECRET" to a happy, peaceful, and abundant life, then YES
- ✓ If you want to learn how to become the "Master of Your Life," then YES
- ✓ If you want to know the "Visualize and Feel" manifestation strategy I used so you can align yourself and be in the receptive mode to receive the abundance waiting for you, then YES

Five things this book will help you achieve:

1. You will learn the concept of Money Growth so that you control money rather than being controlled by it.
2. You will learn how to build wealth while utilizing tax mitigation strategies.
3. You will elevate your knowledge, gain confidence, and expand your vocabulary.
4. You will learn concepts and strategies from a 20+ year experienced CPA/JD with licenses in Insurance, Series 7, and Real Estate.
5. You will increase your influence and earn prestige by sharing knowledge learned here.

Suggestions on how to get the most out of this book:

1. Keep an open mind. You may think that you learned everything you need to learn about a topic, but I am sure you will pick up some things you didn't know before. Do not rush through this book. If you read something that triggers an action item, be sure to stop and write it down in the back of this book so you can go back and execute the action item.
2. This is not a school textbook, so don't expect vast coverage for each topic. Certain concepts and terminologies are introduced here to serve as a guide in developing your strategy.
3. The goal of this book is to also decrease the percentage of financially uneducated people. If you love this book, gift a copy to others and talk about what you learned.

What I didn't know hurt me

I didn't realize until recently when I was invited to attend a workshop that there are financial strategies which I was not aware of, so immediately I thought, if I have a degree in Accounting, and I don't know this, then how many more people are out there lacking this knowledge? Without understanding financial concepts, people are not equipped to make decisions related to their financial management. I wished I had known much sooner, but my focus was not on finance. I was busy raising my son as a Single Mom while working in a highly competitive work environment requiring minimum annual chargeable hours.

There was a survey done by Standard & Poor's Ratings Services Global Financial Literacy based on interviews with more than 150,000 adults in over 140 countries. The result show 57% of adults in the US are financially literate, compared to 33% of adults worldwide. This means that around 3.5 billion adults globally lack an understanding of basic financial concepts.

Norway has the most adults who are financially literate at 71% while Yemen has the least number of adults who are financially literate at 13%. Worldwide, 35% of men and 30% of women are financially literate. Financial literacy was measured using questions assessing basic knowledge of four fundamental concepts in financial decision making: knowledge of interest rates, interest compounding, inflation, and risk diversification. The Council for Economic Education conducts a comprehensive analysis of the K-12 economic and financial education in the United States every two years. They collect data from all 50 states and the District of Columbia. According to the 2020 survey, 21 states require high school students to take a course in personal finance, an increase of 4 states since 2018. The District of Columbia and 5 states still do not include personal finance in their education standards. We are slightly improving but we still have a lot of work to do.

CHAPTER 1
THE UNCOVERING

Belief System

Have you heard these phrases before? "Money doesn't grow on trees," "Money is the root of all evil," "Money doesn't buy happiness," etc.? It was not until a few years ago when I realized that I had these mental blockages, negative patterns, negative programming, limiting beliefs, and subconscious negativity about money. Before I made this realization, I always wondered why I was not able to increase my income. I used to think that I have a long shot at achieving the wealth I desired because I am an Asian female. Little did I know that my words and the way I think of myself were the reasons why I was not able to increase my income. Part of me thought that because I am a minority, I have a long shot no matter how hard I work and no matter how many degrees I have. Then I remember reading my Mom's journal a long time ago where she wrote: "If others can, why can't I?"

I asked that question of myself in January 2018 when I lost my corporate job. That was my fourth layoff. It was meant to happen, otherwise, I wouldn't be where I am. The layoffs were blessings in disguise because after that fourth time, I was determined to never work for anyone else again. And you know what they say, "When the student is ready, the teacher will appear". This is when my business journey began. Since I had gotten my health/life insurance license in late 2017, I decided to utilize it. For the first time in my life, I had to learn the sales cycle, networking, all sorts of marketing strategies, etc. I worked for various insurance companies and learned door to door sales and cold calling techniques. There were times when I asked myself, "Why am I doing this when I can easily find a job utilizing my degrees and my Big 4 public accounting experience"? There were times when I felt sorry for myself, but I was determined to make it, to work for myself no matter what. And just like everything else, after a while, you'll get used to doing things. Little did I know that cold calling and door knocking was a way for me to build character. I was proud of myself for being able to do that because that was outside of my comfort zone. I enjoyed working for insurance companies because I was learning new things. I learned different financial strategies applicable to all ages, even for babies. I was fascinated with everything I learned, but at the same time, curious if others know these strategies. Later, I realized that not a lot of people know about finances. As soon as I became aware of my poverty mindset, my negative self-talk, and my limiting beliefs, I immediately made a paradigm shift. I watched what I said about myself. I changed my relationship with money.

I started loving money. I told myself that it's okay to love money because this will allow me to have a lot of options and do what I am passionate about, traveling and, helping people. I also learned that if I focus on my passion and give back to others without expecting anything in return, everything will fall into place and that's exactly what happened. People, circumstances, and events showed up in my life to help me accomplish my goals.

Of course, all of these did not happen overnight. It took a lot of learning from videos, books, and meditations to change my beliefs and get to the place where I am currently in my spiritual journey. I have a daily routine that I follow consistently. I meditate for an hour in the morning and an hour at night. I practice Vipassana meditation (a technique I used that helps me maintain an equanimous mind and grows compassion for all beings.) I keep a gratitude journal. I recite "I AM" affirmations daily. I have a vision board, so I am clear on what I want to manifest. I practice gratitude whenever I can and only do things that are high vibrational activities. This is important because it is at this level when we are receptive and can manifest things easily, because LIKE attracts LIKE. Have you heard stories of lottery winners who won a substantial amount of money but later end up filing bankruptcy? It's possible that they have negative programming or limiting beliefs that led them to lose everything. How is your relationship with money? Could your limiting beliefs be hindering you from being financially free or thinking big?

There are different ways to release blockages. I ended up taking a course to learn about this. I learned how to connect with the source of energy, expand my energy which helped heal my beliefs from past lives and any poverty consciousness. I deleted, I canceled, and destroyed all my limiting beliefs across all dimensions, lifetimes, space, plains of existence, consciousness, realities, and beyond. Then I replaced them with positive energies and vibrations. Did I lose you already? It's okay, you were probably not expecting to hear an analytical person like me talk about this topic.

I want you to pause for a minute and think about your beliefs about money because unless you are aware that you have blockages, you don't know to fix them, right?

So, here are some of the questions that I asked my client mentees:

Do you have a belief that money is the root of all evil?

Do you have a belief that it is unspiritual to want money?

Do you have a belief that it's wrong to have money when other people don't?

Do you feel shame and guilt when it comes to talking about money?

Do you feel uncomfortable when talking about money?

Do you feel that you never have enough money?

Do you worry about not having any money?

Do members of your family fight a lot about money?

What are some of the phrases you hear about money when you were growing up?

Unless you have already released your money blockages before, it's highly likely that you have to clear them for the first time. If you have already cleared them before, and you're still not getting positive results, then perhaps you may have to clear them a few more times. At least, you now know that you have them, and you will have to pay attention to how you act, how you feel, and what you say about money. If you don't like money, it's not going to come to you. That's the bottom line. You must be comfortable handling and talking about money.

Reset Button

We should be grateful that there's such a thing as the "RESET" button we can choose to press any time we want. We can start over again whenever we choose to. It's called free will. Whether you have formal education or not, your belief system plays an important role in your success, and no matter where you are in life or your financial life cycle, you can hit that reset button and transform. No one else is responsible for our financial health but us. My favorite quote from Benjamin Franklin says: "If you fail to plan, you are planning to fail." In Napoleon Hill's Think and Grow Rich, the sixth of the 13 principles is to plan. Unfortunately, not a lot of people do it. Perhaps they don't know how, or they don't think they'll need to, or they think they can rely on the government or their job. Well, you can cross out that last one because we are living in a different generation, unlike the earlier generations where people stayed in one job forever. I remember being looked at differently in my earlier career because I changed jobs every couple of years. For some people back then, that was not normal. The last job was the longest job I kept. I was there for a little over 8 years, and the only reason is that I was able to move around departments three times. Moving jobs a lot was not normal. Times have changed.

Albert Einstein said, "Insanity is doing the same thing over and over again and expecting different results." We hear this all the time, but we still see people not take action. Why? Is it a lack of will power? Is it because it is hopeless to think that things will ever change? Is it because they don't know how? Is it because their environment is not conducive to positive thinking? Is it because family members will just put them down with their desire to change? Is it because they're waiting for their spouse or kids or children to change?

The only prerequisite to fix this is that you must want to change. You must have the will power to change. You must have a strong determination to change. You must have a compelling reason to change. So, I want you to pause for a minute to think about this one. Do you want to change your current financial condition or your current health condition or your current relationship? If so, write down why. What would be the steps you have to take to make the change? Write it down. How would you feel after you implement those changes? Would you gain more confidence? Would you be happy? Would you feel accomplished? Keep this mental picture in your head and feel the emotion as a result of your achievement.

What I had you do just now is a manifestation exercise which I call the "Visualize and Feel" strategy. Did you know that everything you want in life is already here? You just have to align yourself, but people don't know how to do it because of negative programming, their surroundings, their fear, their worry, their doubts, and all the negative thoughts one can think of. Those are what I call, the "Abundance Blockers". The moment you feel negative, you are moving far away from your desires, wishes, and dreams. That's why I always tell my client mentees to be aware of what they say, do, feel, and act. I ask that you do the same. Pay close attention and observe because you might have a poverty mindset from another lifetime that you may be carrying in this life that you are not even aware of.

My wish is that I hear from you, to let me know what actions you took which helped you achieve your goals. I also wish that this book will inspire you to create multi-generational wealth for your family because you can. You have the power to. You just don't know it because you're too busy watching fake news, binging on Netflix, scrolling on Instagram photos and vids, checking out new Tweets, checking what everyone on Facebook is doing on a Saturday night, watching countless music vids on TikTok or playing online games. And people wonder why their financial situation hasn't improved, right? So, pay attention to what you are doing every day. Unless the things you do are contributing to your ultimate goal, unless you're a stockholder of those internet companies, you're just making other people rich so, use your 24 hours wisely and effectively.

Always remember that you are an abundant being, it's just that your programming had been altered because of the society we live in, limiting beliefs passed down from generations, and events that may have happened in your life which made you think the way you do. Once you are aware of this, then you can transform. However, you must want to make the change. That's the prerequisite.

Napoleon Hill said: "Whatever the mind can conceive and believe, the mind can achieve". Some of you will take heed of this, and some of you will not. But what have you got to lose if you believe? Try it. Picture this. Imagine someone who has formal university education who believes he can only make a certain amount of money because there's a maximum amount of salary for his specific profession versus someone who doesn't have a formal university education but believes that the sky is the limit when it comes to income. Who do you think will most likely be a billionaire? Who are the famous wealthy people who did not finish college but have done very well? There are several of them. They are the ones who knew how to leverage, delegate, use their imaginative skills and creativity. They hire coaches and mentors to guide them. They hire professionals who are smarter than them and pay them just enough so that they don't leave. Which side do you want to be on?

Reward System

There are so many excellent books out there that teach about personal finance and wealth creation but how come, the percentage of financially uneducated is still so high at 67% worldwide? My determination to write this book is partly because of that statistic.

I see no reason why we should have that many people who are not doing well in the financial area. I don't think the education part is the only problem. I think the execution part is also an issue. Maybe people do not have goals, or if they have goals, they don't know how to make them happen. Maybe it's their money blockages that hinder them from the abundant life that's waiting for them. That's why I came up with this idea that perhaps rewarding people will provide that little push that they need.

I was raised in a household where parents reward children for doing well in school and it worked. I also applied this reward system to my son's education. Grades A's and B's had a certain dollar value. Grade C was neutral. Grades D's, and F's, meant he had to pay me. Thank God he only got A's and B's, otherwise, my strategy would not have worked. When I reward myself, I use travel, because travel is my passion. I work hard and reward myself by going on annual trips to places I have never been to.

Unfortunately, as a U.S. employee, vacation days are so limited – the max you can get is 2 to 4 weeks, and depending on what you do for a living, you may not be able to take consecutive weeks off. If you are a CPA with tax clients, you're not only busy during tax season, you're busy year-round because you have clients who have fiscal year ends. Looking back, I couldn't believe I did 11 years of public accounting. Funny thing is, the Universe tried to get me out of the situation, but I didn't know any better. If only I had known then what I know now, I would've gotten out so much sooner. Anyway, when I lost my job in 2018, traveling was the first thing I did. Some would think that it was a crazy move, that I should have been saving my money but that is a "lack" mindset. I went on vacation for one month and it was the longest vacation I ever had since I started working at age 16. I was able to visit relatives in four countries in Europe: Spain, Italy, England, and Scotland. Before that year ended, I went to Asia for a month. But the most memorable trip was the luxurious cruise with Regent Seven Seas to Alaska in 2016 and visited five cities: Ketchikan, Juneau, Skagway, Sitka, and Seward. That was my second cruise to Alaska. If you haven't been, you should go. Take Regent Seven Seas, you'll be spoiled.

Why am I saying these things? Well, because I want to give away luxury trips. It will be fun, and it will be my way of inspiring and motivating people to take action. I like contests and raffles. I always win gifts here and there. It's fun winning. I want others to experience that. Give my readers a chance to join us in our annual business conferences at luxurious resorts around the world. The idea is for people to think big. I want people to learn how to use their manifestation powers to get what they want. Wouldn't it be fun if they can practice manifesting this trip? The eligibility rules to participate will be detailed later.

This pandemic put a toll on my travel plans. I was supposed to be out of the country all of August, but it didn't happen due to COVID 19. The next annual business conference will be on the anniversary of this book launch in 2021. The first trip will be to a private island paradise of Amanpulo. Why there? Because it's an Aman resort and it's located in the Philippines, my home country. It would be great to have them generate tourism revenue from this event.

This private island can only be reached by a private plane and it is about an hour from Manila. Amanpulo is encircled by pearl-white sand and turquoise waters of the Sulu sea. When we get there, we can fill our days with aquatic adventures from kite surfing, scuba diving, snorkeling, paddleboarding, kayaking, sea bobbing, sunset cruising, fishing expeditions, helicopter excursions, or on-shore activities like cycling, bird watching, star gazing, and jungle obstacle course. We can experience an afternoon snack at the sandbar, enjoy the drinks at the Kawayan bar (it's a floating bar made of bamboo), or the pristine coral reefs stretching over seven square kilometers start just 200 meters from the island's sandy shores. This island is also a nesting site for green and hawksbill turtles and watching turtle hatchlings emerge from their nests and make their way to the ocean would be a magical experience. By the way, I am not getting paid for advertising Aman resorts, I simply want to show you how you should train your mind to imagine the life you desire. You will understand this better when I explain the "Visualize and Feel" manifestation strategy.

It would be great to meet the people I impacted with this book, and that's why I'm opening up our annual business conference to others on a first come first serve basis. I want my readers to share their success stories and join me in my mission to motivate and inspire others. These are the luxury resorts in the pipeline. Is it obvious that I'm deprived of my travels due to the pandemic? Here are my top picks: Soneva Jani (Maldives), Six Senses Zil Pasyon (Seychelles), Qualia Great Barrier Reef (Australia), 12 Apostles Hotel (South Africa), Four Seasons Hualalai (Hawaii), St. Regis Bora Bora, Amanyara (Turks & Caicos), Soneva Kiri (Thailand), The Wickaninnish Inn (Canada), Shangri La Boracay (Philippines), and Four Seasons Kuda Huraa (Maldives).

It's always good to look forward to something fun. At least, that's how I motivate myself to accomplish the goals I set. Work hard, play hard!

Emotional Quotient (EQ) vs Intelligence Quotient (IQ)

What do EQ and IQ have to do with personal finance,? First, let me ask you this, why do some smart people make the same dumb mistakes?

Let's define and differentiate EQ from IQ. Diffen.com defined EQ as an individual's ability to identify, evaluate, control, and express emotions. IQ on the other hand is a score derived from one of the several standardized tests designed to assess an individual's intelligence. It is the ability to learn, understand, and apply information to skills, logical reasoning, word comprehension, math skills, and filter irrelevant information.

Here's another definition of EQ, "it's the ability to process painful emotions in healthy and effective ways." Someone with a high EQ would deal with the emotions of losing a valued job in healthy and effective ways such as acknowledging the feelings and practicing self-care. On the other hand, someone with a low EQ would deal with the same situation in ineffective and self-destructive ways like drinking, taking drugs, hopelessness, denial, avoidance, emotional eating, etc.

Another definition of IQ is, "the ability to learn and use one's thinking mind to skillfully solve problems. Someone with a high IQ will be skilled at solving problems through learning and reasoning. Someone with a high IQ will learn how to use a computer program efficiently while someone with a lower IQ would find that task more difficult. So how can those smart people with high IQ avoid making the same dumb mistakes? They must learn to identify the strong emotional needs and low EQ strategies that perpetuate the mistakes and then replace them with high EQ skills that deal with the emotional pain in effective and healthy ways.

Our emotions influence our money decisions and it is as important as the technical aspect of money. This is the reason why in the beginning, I talked about your belief system and how you feel about money because you can learn the financial know-how easily but if you're not comfortable about money then it will be hard to build wealth if that's your goal.

Allow me to tell you a story of a friend who is very analytical and has an extremely high IQ, but not really in touch with his emotions. This individual is an authority in his field. Recently he started using the power of emotional intelligence after he realized that he had a lot of missed opportunities in the past because he didn't know to trust his intuition. For example, several years ago there was a start-up entertainment company that offered him an opportunity to join their team but he didn't accept it because they are just starting at that time and the business idea didn't appeal to him. Years later, the same company went public and this company is now very profitable in the industry. He could have made a lot of money, but he based his decision not to join using his intellectual mind and he probably rationalized everything else. I wouldn't be surprised if he prepared a pros and cons spreadsheet whether to join or not to join, something that an analytical person would do. Another opportunity was presented to him, and the same thing happened. He did not join the company before its initial public offering (IPO) and that was another missed opportunity. By the way, those two companies are Netflix and Google. Moral of the story: you cannot simply rely on your intellectual abilities in making important decisions. Use both EQ and IQ.

There was an article published by CNBC where they reported that 44% of Americans surveyed would rather discuss death, religion, or politics than talk about personal finance with a loved one and the two major reasons are fear of conflict and embarrassment. Then there was another survey done where 50% of the first marriages end in divorce, and financial conflict is often a key contributor. The article also added that, in our society, it's considered rude to discuss money and wealth. Now we know, why we have 43% of financially uneducated people in the U.S.

FINRA's Investor Education Foundation discovered a clear decline in financial literacy over the past nine years. In 2009, 42% of respondents were able to answer 4 or more questions correctly in a five-question survey on fundamental concepts of economics and personal finance. By 2018, this dropped 8 percentage points to 34%. More alarming, less than 1/3 of adults understand three basic financial literacy topics by age 40, even though many important financial decisions have already been made when they were much younger.

My hope is that this book will empower the readers especially those who are parents and teachers, to share their thoughts and feelings about spending, saving, and investing money with their children. If we don't have this discussion with our children, who will? We cannot rely on our school system. Our society programmed us to think poor so people will stay poor. If the government wanted the people to be financially educated, they would have changed the school system already to include personal finance as part of the curriculum in all high schools.

If people understood how inflation, rate of return, and how tax affect their money, no one would ever put their money in the savings account in their banks. The government will never want that to happen because banks will lose customers and bank shareholders will not be happy. There is a smarter way to build wealth, but most people don't want to listen when someone tries to educate them. People think they know it all. That's what I thought until that one day that I sat in the financial workshop.

The "REAL" Secret

Did you know there are 50 Laws of the Universe? Wow, I didn't realize this until recently. For a long time, I only knew one from the book, "The Secret," which everyone knows (Law of Attraction) and then I came across the Law of Vibration and then Quantum Physics which led me to the other laws. I am not going to try to explain Quantum Physics because I don't even know how to begin, but I found this definition for beginners from sciencedaily.com that states, "Quantum mechanic is a physical science dealing with the behavior of matter and energy on the scale of atoms and subatomic particles/waves". Did you get that? Probably not, but it's okay, we'll go through the different laws, and hopefully by the time we're done with this topic, you'll understand the concept. When you understand these universal laws, I think that you will think twice about feeling negative or have ill will towards others ever again. At least, that's how this affected me. These laws provide us with a blueprint for how we can live our best life. So, take a step back and observe how your life is right now.

If you are encountering obstacles or you feel lost, frustrated, and confused about what your life purpose is, it's probably because you still don't understand the connections between the Spiritual Laws, which means you are probably going against the flow. I will do my best to explain these laws which are based on metaphysical, philosophical, and quantum physics principles.

Do you believe that you can create your reality? It's true. Quantum Physics already proves this, but people still question it instead of believing that it can happen. We are all governed by a set of Universal Laws.

These are laws created by GOD to aid us in creating the life we desire. So, could this be the REAL secret that the 1% are not letting others know? Yes, possibly. Why was this information not out there? Why aren't people talking about this? Why did they only show one law, the Law of Attraction? I am so fascinated by discovering this. Having a good understanding of how these Universal Laws affects your reality will help you stay positive and will give you a better understanding of metaphysics (a branch of philosophy that deals with the first principles of things i.e. being, knowing, substance, cause, identity, time, and space). Honestly, I had questions about life in general which these laws answered for me. This is an example of, "Seek and you will find, knock and the door will be opened to you."

"Suffering Mitigation" Tip

We are conditioned to believe that things exist only if we can see, feel, taste, hear, or touch them. We disregard anything else that is beyond the perception of these five senses but whether we believe it or not, these Universal Laws affect our reality, and this can never be changed because it is the law. When we work within these laws, we will end up with a positive outcome and if we work outside these laws, we will end up suffering, but only to teach us until we learn. Hopefully, we don't make the same mistake over and over again.

When we understand these laws, then we can go through life with less suffering or no suffering at all.

As I look back during the times when I got laid off four times, I remember that I couldn't help but think that maybe there is something wrong with me. I was questioning whether I was good enough. Was it my color, or my age, or gender? Perhaps if I was more spiritual when it happened the second time, I would have known to look further and seek what the Universe wanted me to do, but I didn't have the spiritual knowledge then. I was religious. I went to church every Sunday but I didn't learn this in church.

Also, I was probably just too busy providing for my son and I was in a highly competitive work environment. It took me, four layoffs to realize that I was going against what the Universe had planned for me. What I was doing was not in alignment with what makes me happy and fulfilled. Don't get me wrong, I like being a CPA as a profession, but I always have a passion for teaching, coaching, and mentoring. I remember growing up, I would tutor my sisters with their homework. In college, I was a Faculty Assistant. When I was working at a CPA firm, I would mentor the staff and now I am a Volunteer Instructor at Score teaching entrepreneurs. What I'm trying to say is, use the knowledge that you learn from this book to help you figure out if you are in alignment with the Universe so you mitigate your suffering and live a harmonious life.

If you wake up every morning and you're not enthusiastic to start working, that means you are not in alignment with your higher self and your life purpose so you have to seek within, connect with the Universe, learn to trust your gut, and your heart. Ask yourself: What do I like doing? What am I passionate about? What makes me happy? Whatever it is, all of us have unique gifts and talents so use that and follow your heart's desire.

The 50 Spiritual Laws of the Universe

If I had come across these Laws of the Universe several years ago, before my spiritual journey, I probably wouldn't understand what they mean. I suggest that before you continue, pause for a minute and ask the Divine/God/Universe/Spirit Guide/Angels, whoever you believe in, to help you understand these laws as this understanding will help you answer some of the questions you may have about life. By understanding the laws, you will have more compassion for others around you because you gained an understanding as far as why they act the way they do. You will lessen your annoyance and aversion about everything because your perspective on things will change. You will be more at peace and happier. Well, at least that's how my spiritual journey and these laws have affected me.

1. **The Law of Harmony.** This law supersedes even the fundamental Law of Karma, for it is the supreme potential of balance. The purpose of karma is to attain harmony. If you throw a rock into a pond, you disturb the harmony of the pond. You are the cause, and the effect is the splash and the ripples that flow out in the back until the harmony is restored. Similarly, your disharmonious karmic actions flow out into the universe and back upon you, lifetime after lifetime until eventually your harmony is restored. So, as you experience your life, you and the entire Universe, are experiencing the karmic ripples which will eventually result in harmony.

When you live the life of harmony you become free from the wheel of reincarnation.

2. **The Law of Reincarnation and Karma.** Until you have resolved your karma and fulfilled your dharma (the principle that orders the Universe), you will continue to reincarnate into sequential lifetimes upon the earth. Neither God nor the Lords of Karma, bestow suffering upon you during these lives. You and you alone, decide what you most need to learn in your earthly sojourn. During your earthly sojourn, you seek out other souls often with shared histories and with karmic configurations matching your needs. Whenever you act with intention you create karma. Actions are thoughts, emotions, words, and deeds, while the motive, desire, and intent lie behind each. Disharmonious acts must be balanced during this life or a future lifetime. They are rooted in fear-based emotions which must be resolved before you can release yourself from the wheel of reincarnation. You return lifetime after lifetime to test yourself to see if you have learned your lessons. Until you can go through an entire lifetime with total involvement and no disharmonious attachment whatsoever, you will continue to reincarnate. When you can live a life of perfect harmony, liberation will follow.

3. **The Law of Wisdom.** Wisdom erases karma. If you have the wisdom to learn your lesson through wisdom and love, you can mitigate your suffering. Sadly though, we seem to learn fastest through pain, when we directly experience the consequences of our actions. When you move toward a predestined test in your life, and you have the wisdom to proceed with harmony, you can mitigate the traumatic impact of the event. For example, in your previous life, you were married to a soul whom you left for another. Before you were born into your current life, you agreed to be left by your mate under the same circumstances. This will allow you to balance your karma and directly experience the pain of abandonment. If through your wisdom and master of life awareness, it would be easy for you to detach from the relationship with love, you will ease the pain of parting while also passing your test. Wisdom will have erased the karma.

4. **The Law of Grace.** Karma can be experienced to the letter of the law, or in mercy and grace. If you give love, mercy, and grace to others, you will receive the same in return. For example, you are destined to experience a future event in which you will be the victim of slander and gossip, which will ruin your career, but in the years preceding this event you have become so kind and loving to other human beings, it is obvious to your higher self that you have

learned your needed lesson so the predestined event will be mitigated with little or no effect upon you.

5. **The Law of Soul Evolution.** Everyone on earth shares the goal of soul evolution whether they realize it or not. We have reincarnated because we desired to spiritually evolve by rising above our fear-based emotions and learning to express unconditional love. In so doing, we raise our vibrational rate and moved closer to a state of harmony. Even when it appears that you may not be evolving, you are, in reality, making progress. We learn through the pain of our disharmonious acts, which can be viewed as our mistakes and failures, but if you fell off a bicycle nine times and you learned on the tenth attempt, you needed nine failures to achieve your success. Every failure was a small success bringing you closer to accomplishing your goal.

6. **The Law of the Bodhisattva.** Bodhisattva is a Sanskrit term commonly accepted by most metaphysical adepts today. It means one who has transcended the need for earthly incarnations but who was chosen to return to the earth to support others in achieving enlightenment. A Bodhisattva knows that he will never be free until all souls are free. Most serious students of metaphysics have entered the bodhisattva development stage of their evolution.

7. **The Law of Vibrational Attainment.** The entire universe operates on the same principle of vibrational energy. When Einstein discovered that matter is energy, he opened the door to merge science with metaphysics. Scientist has proven that energy cannot die, it can only transform. And by its very nature, energy must move forward or backward, then still. Stagnation results in transformation. You are energy. Your skin which appears solid is trillions of swiftly moving molecules orbiting each other at a specific vibrational rate, a physical life rate that you earned in the past as a result of how harmoniously or disharmoniously you've lived in your past lives and your current life up until this very moment in time.

8. **The Law of Free Will.** This law operates in three ways: (1) Although many of the major events in your life are astrologically predestined, you always have free will to mitigate the impact of the event or to transcend it entirely. This will result from how you live your life up to the situation you have destined for yourself to experience.

If you give grace and mercy to others, are positive, loving, compassionate, and demonstrate by your actions that you have learned past lessons, you can minimize disharmonious experiences. (2) As you maintained the master of life awareness and develop conscious attachment, you will be far less affected by worldly events than in the past. A master of life enjoys all the warmth and joy that life has to offer but detaches from the negativity by allowing it to flow through him without affecting him. (3) You always have free will in how you respond to any situation. If you respond with positive emotions, compassion, and integrity you have probably learned your karmic lessons and will not have to experience a similar situation in the future.

9. **The Law of One.** Every soul living in discarnate is connected at the level of the collective unconscious, deep within the higher self. We are all part of the energy gestalt of God and because we are a part of God, we are God. It is the goal of the gestalt to move the energy forward creating more energy. So, in living harmoniously, we each increase our vibrational rate and intensify the vibration of the entire gestalt. When we are disharmonious, we decrease the vibration of the entire gestalt. Because we are one, everything we think, say, and do, as well as the motive, intent, and desire behind our actions, affects every other soul.

10. **The Law of Manifestation.** Everything manifest begins as a thought, an idea. Ideas and experiences create beliefs, which in turn create reality. If you are unhappy with your current reality, you must change your beliefs and your behavior. Beliefs can be changed when you recognize that they are not working for you and begin programming what will create success and harmony in your life. The unlimited creative power of your mind, through dedication, awareness, and training can be the wisdom to rise above your karma. Within the physical laws, you can manifest any reality you desire to experience. Regarding changing your behavior, you must decide which disharmonious behaviors you want to eliminate. Then be aware that you don't have to change how you feel about something to affect it if you are willing to change what you were doing.

11. **The Law of Conscious Detachment.** Buddha's earthly teachings are best summarized by one of his statements, "It is your resistance to what is, that causes you suffering". By suffering, he meant everything that doesn't work in your life such as relationship problems, loss of loved ones, loneliness, sickness, accidents, guilt, monetary hardship, unfulfilled desires, etc. When you accept what

is, you accept the unalterable realities in your life without resisting them. Some things are facts; they exist no matter how much you resist. There is nothing you can do about it. Change what you can change but have the wisdom to accept unalterable situations as they are without wasting mental or physical energy attempting to change what you cannot change. Out of this acceptance, comes involved detachment. The ability to enjoy all the positive aspects of life but to allow the negativity to flow through you without resistance and without affecting you.

12. **The Law of Gratitude.** From the perspective of karma and The Law of One, the more you give the more you will receive. The more you assist others, the more you assist yourself. The power of this law also works in your day to day life.

13. **The Law of Fellowship.** When two or more people of similar vibrations are gathered for a shared purpose, their combined energy directed to the attainment of that purpose is doubled, tripled, quadrupled, or more. This esoteric awareness has been used by esoteric religions, healing groups, and worldwide meditations for peace.

14. **The Law of Resistance.** That which you resist, you draw to you and you will perpetuate its influence upon your life. Resistance is fear, so it isn't karmically resolved. The law of resistance assures that you let go of the fear by encountering it until you are forced to deal with it by learning conscious detachment. For example, you are extremely resistant to your mother in law, resulting in constant conflicts with her. When you attain a master of life awareness and stop resisting her by consciously detaching from the negativity, the problem will be resolved. Most disharmonious situations are solved through a change in viewpoint. By changing your perspective, you can usually eliminate the effects of a problem. If you're no longer affected by a problem, you no longer have a problem even when nothing about the problematic situation may have changed. That which you resist, you become, if not in this lifetime, in the future reincarnation. Another example would be if you have a strong resistance toward people of the Asian race. Your resistance is fear and the quickest way to overcome fear is to directly experience what you find so fearful, thus you will reincarnate as an Asian in the future lifetime.

15. **The Law of Attraction.** Where your attention goes, your energy flows. You attract what you are and what you concentrate upon. If you are negative, you draw in and experience negativity.

If you are loving, you draw in and experience love. You can only attract to you those qualities you possess. If you want peace and harmony in your life, you must become peaceful and harmonious.

16. **The Law of Reflection.** The traits you respond to in others, you recognize in yourself, both positive and negative. It has four primary manifestations: (1) That which you admire in others you recognize as existing within yourself. (2) That which you resist in others and react to strongly in others is sure to be found within yourself. (3) That which you fear in others is something which you are afraid that exists in you. (4) That which you resist in yourself, you will dislike in others. Your goal is to let go of fear so you can open yourself up for more unconditional love.

17. **The Law of Unconditional Love.** The expression of unconditional love will eventually result in harmony. Unconditional love is not romantic love. It is the acceptance of others without judgment or expectations. It's the total acceptance of others without an attempt to change the law of unconditional love. If you go out of your way to express unconditional love, you automatically rise above fear. As you transcend your fear, you automatically open to the expression of unconditional love.

18. **Law of Magnetic Affinities.** By astrologically choosing the time and place of your birth, you determine the nature and the effects and experience in your life. On the other side, before you were born, you made decisions about the life you would enter into. You chose your parents, other souls to interact with you, and the astrological configurations of your birth which determined your character, personality, abilities, restrictions, and timing for strengths and weaknesses. Be aware that you are only using 5 to 10 percent of the capacity of your brain.

19. **The Law of Abundance.** You have within yourself everything required to make your earthly incarnation a paradise if you choose to accept that which is your natural birthright. We live in a Universe of abundance although the majority of those populating our planet appear to view it as a Universe of scarcity.

20. **The Law of Divine Order.** If you seek to understand the law of Divine order, study the natural balance of nature. There are no accidents. Your energy translated into thoughts, words, emotions, and deeds causes all your experiences. This assures that you always have the learning opportunities you require to resolve your karma. The collective thoughts, words, emotions, and deeds of mankind create the environment for us all. If enough souls focus their energy

upon peace, we will have peace. If the majority of souls are filled with anger, we may all have to experience war. We are all one, but just like the many sub-personalities within you, the dominant traits of mankind will emerge to resolve our group karma. As always, fear is the problem and love is the answer.

21. **Law of Attitude.** Nothing in the Universe can harm you but your attitude. It is your attitude that moves you toward events and experiences and it is your attitude that worsens or lightens any event, catastrophe, or tragedy. You, and you alone, choose the attitude with which you will respond. No two people would respond to the situation in the same way. Every earthly incarnation includes traumatic experiences and the better you understand the working of karma, the more likely you put events with a spiritual perspective.

22. **The Law of Threes.** Two is generally recognized as positive and negative and it becomes a law when it is combined with a neutralizing force. When three become a unit, neither of the original two is more powerful or larger and each behaves itself as a benefit of the whole. For example, father, son, and holy ghost. Conscious, subconscious, and super-conscious. Mother, father, and child. When a man and woman combined with the neutralizing state of marriage, they become a three.

23. **The Law of Association.** If two or more units have something in common, the commonality can be used to influence or control the other thing. The amount of control depends upon the degree of commonality. The more in common they both are, the more the influence. For example, if you pray while holding a Bible, you will be more likely to experience a spiritual connectedness. The Bible and prayer share a commonality.

24. **The Law of Commitment.** When you become clear on your intent, making a decision, and obligating yourself to a task or a belief, everything will begin to fall into place if your direction is in harmony with the Universe as it relates to your purpose. The key to this power is not to have indecisiveness at all, and the more your emotional desire the more power you give to those on the other side who can assist you more rapidly than manifestation.

25. **The Law of Dissonance.** You are going to experience mental discomfort when you hold two conflicting beliefs or when your actions do not agree with your beliefs. For example, if you believe that smoking is bad for your health, yet you continue to smoke.

You believe extramarital affairs are morally wrong, and yet you continued to be involved with people outside your marriage. You believed that you should be a patient mother, yet you continue to yell at your children. The law says that when your beliefs and actions are incompatible, you will attempt to reduce the resulting discomfort by changing either your actions or your beliefs. The smoker will become an ex-smoker, or he will deny or rationalize the health threat. The adulteress will either stop or rationalize her actions by saying, what my husband doesn't know won't hurt him, and besides, when my needs are fulfilled, I am a better wife. The impatient mother changes her behavior or rationalizes her attitude by saying, it's better for me to yell and release the anger than repress my emotions. The Law of Dissonance is sometimes called the Law of Self Delusion.

26. **The Law of Experience.** New information entering your mind destroys previous information of a similar nature once a pathway of information has been established in your brain. That viewpoint will prevail unless new information comes in to destroy and replace it. For example, if you fall off a horse and hurt yourself, and that's the end of your experience with horses, your experience has been programmed negatively. That's why instructors always encourage riders to climb back on the horse immediately after falling off. You need new fresh input to erase the trauma of the fall. Also, note that the subconscious mind cannot tell the difference between fantasies and real experiences. For example, if you experience extreme anxiety around crowds, in an altered state, you can vividly imagine yourself perfectly relaxed in a crowd of people. Your mind will accept this as a reality and invoke the law of experience. After a few days, weeks, or months of this programming, your mind will experience calm in crowds and it will carry over into your personal reality.

27. **The Law of Fearful Confrontation.** If you fear doing something and yet have the courage to do it anyway, you will soon do a mental flip flop and may even become addicted to doing it. For example, if you fear sky diving but forced yourself to do it, the experience could generate the internal release of beta-endorphins. These internally manufactured opioids chemically resembled opium and are quite addicting. The more you skydive, the more you will want to skydive or ski or gamble or whatever it was that you originally feared, and it causes you this internal rush.

28. **The Law of Group Consciousness.** Every one of us is part of a great energy gestalt and connected in the level of collective

unconsciousness. Each individual aspect of the gestalt has its own electrical system, its own vibrational frequency, and interacts with all other aspects. We are all electrically connected to one another and to a certain point. On a higher self of psychic level, it is possible to tune in to anyone else and to draw upon the awareness of the entire gestalt.

29. **The Law of Personal Return.** This law is another way to view karma, some people prefer it. If you think negatively of someone or send hateful thoughts to them, the thoughts may harm the person, but in due course, they will return to the sender as sent. The same is true for disharmonious deeds. The good news is, the law of personal return also works in reverse. The positive acts, words, and deeds will be returned to the sender.

30. **The Law of Activity.** Action is a result of thought and part of a triad. Every thought produces an alchemical process in your consciousness and is the manifestation of motive, intent, or desire, this union of two is necessary for action and will ordain the karmic implications.

31. **The Law of Denial.** When you refuse to deal with a highly emotional issue or refuse to take responsibility for an unpleasant situation, you avoid living up to your potential. Such things can be put off for a lifetime, but the effect will be experienced mentally and physically, or as a lifestyle manifestation until you correctly fix the situation.

32. **The Law of New Beginnings.** It says we all have major life turning points. There is a break in the energy wave pattern and a complete change will result. Everything is affected by this change and flux, some things to a lesser degree than others. An example would be a traumatic tragedy such as (1) the death of a loved one, (2) a religious conversion, (3) a point in therapy when something clicks and from that time on the patient begins to get well, and (4) a mother giving birth to a baby.

33. **Law of Compensation.** It says that you and you alone are responsible for everything that happens to you. All is the result of your past thoughts, words, and deeds which form your present attitude. Your attitude towards life and life experiences has returned to you in a form of reward, problems, as love and joy, or as confusion and trouble, as well as heartbreaking experience. This karmic rewards and punishments can be delivered immediately, later in your present life, or in a future reincarnation.

34. **Law of Psychometric Influence.** It says that two things, animate and inanimate once in contact with each other will continue to act upon each other even at a distance long after the actual contact had been severed. Matter encountering the other matter absorbs an influence as a result of the contact. There is a psychometric blending of the etheric emanations, thus the person wearing a piece of inherited jewelry will be influenced by the psychometric emanation of the original owner. The more empathic the person is, the more likely she will be influenced by the state of mind of the original owner.

35. **The Law of Totality.** It says that each part of totality has its own characteristics, and also takes on the characteristics of the totality as a sum of its parts. Each part has two functions, to retain its own characteristics and to function as part of the totality. When separated, each part remains in contact with the totality. And because it retains the character of the totality, it can perform as the totality. You may not realize this yet but since you are part of God, you contain the potential to perform as God. This law is often expressed as the Law of One.

36. **The Law of Dominant Desire.** It says that the stronger emotion will always dominate a weaker one. It doesn't matter which idea you consciously favor, or even know to be desirable, the stronger emotion will nullify the weaker ones and the strongest emotion will begin to permeate all aspects of your activity.

37. **The Law of Duality.** It says that the Universe and all energy function as a yin yang balance resulting in a tension between the opposites. Yin is negative. Yang is positive. We all contain this dual aspect expressed as love and hate, harmony, and chaos, good and evil. This tension is necessary for the structure to exist and human beings are energy structures. In relating this to your life, you must realize that without tension you don't exist thus there is a need for yin balance in your life. Some people express their yin energy in undesirable ways such as self-denial, excess hard work, gambling, dangerous activity, or arguing or fighting. Sickness and war are an expression of yin energy.

38. **The Law of Self Destruction.** It says, as a natural expression of the Law of Duality, that which is successful tends to destroy itself. So, do not dare to allow your relationship, your career, your spirituality to become successful. You realized, if you reached that pinnacle, you greatly increased the potential for self-destruction. An example would be a successful business executive who makes

it to the top of his profession, then has a mid-life identity crisis or a nervous breakdown and destroys it all. Once total success was obtained, there was no more challenge, and destruction followed. Unless you challenge yourself, you will stagnate. Remember, you are energy and stagnation is self-destruction. Energy cannot standstill. It must by its very nature move forward or backward, so instead of holding back, attain total success but not complacency. Always give yourself great new challenges. If you let the challenge go too far, self-destruction is the result. If you don't incorporate challenges in your life, self-destruction is the result. If you keep a challenging balance, you succeed in maintaining your position and retaining your success. The secret is to consciously direct challenge in a way that minimizes jeopardy while fulfilling the yin yang need of balance. This will usually accomplish by wise risk-taking.

39. **The Law of Environmental Manifestation.** It says that everything that surrounds you is an extension of you i.e. your mate, your home, your furnishings, your car, your pets, your yard, your office, and your career, are a physical expression of attitudes and belief system. Your environment is a real picture of your core beliefs and expresses your self-image and your cultural overview.

40. **The Law of Restriction.** It says that man cannot create anything higher than his own level of understanding thus society can never get any better than the level of mankind as a whole. We must work from the inside out. Every one of us on this planet can incorporate the power of harmonious thinking which is the only long-term solution to poverty and limitation. To heal the world, we must each first heal ourselves.

41. **The Law of Self Worth.** It says that you can only attract to you, that which you feel worthy of. Your self-esteem is critical to your happiness and success. The truth is, you are not what you have, and you are not what you do. Beneath your fear programming, you are perfect and an enlightened soul, fully self-actualized, and a living example of unconditional love. It is only lifetimes of fear programming that are keeping you from acknowledging who you are. The more you can let go of your fear, the higher your self-esteem and, the more options you will have, and the more risk you can take. The better you like yourself the better others will like you and the more worthy you will feel.

42. **The Law of Growth.** It says that there is no growth without discontent. You know what is best for you and you will strive for more awareness.

Never allow yourself to reach a level of self-satisfaction where there is no new challenge. For most of us, there will be no growth if there's no agitation or discontent so carefully study your dissatisfaction for it will tell you what you're about to leave behind and possibly point to a new future direction. Make sure the future is one of happiness and success.

43. **The Law of Self Truth.** It says that truth is what works for you. If you believe something to be, it becomes a truth for you. The idea is to be careful of what you accept, for it will influence all aspects of your life and your future.

44. **The Law of Summarized Experience.** It says that you are the total of all that has happened to you in this life that you are now living, and all of your past. Everything from your health, your relationships, your sexual experiences, your career standing, and everything else can be used as a barometer to show who you are.

45. **The Law of Belief.** It says you can have anything you want if you can give up the belief that you can't have it, as long as what you want doesn't conflict with someone else's belief. In the area of accomplishment, you must achieve the education necessary to create what you want. So, this is the area on which to focus your desirous energy.

46. **The Law of Dharmic Direction.** It says that you have within you a guiding principle which is your duty to yourself and society. The secret is to listen to your inner direction which will direct you to fulfill your dharma and resolve your karma.

47. **The Law of Purifying Action.** It says that by living the three pillars of dharma you will spiritually evolve. The first pillar of dharma is generosity, meaning non-greed, letting go. The second pillar of dharma is moral strength which includes five basic precepts, not killing, not stealing, not committing sexual misconduct, not using wrong speech, not taking intoxicants that could cloud the mind and make it dull. The third pillar of dharma is meditation and it covers two areas: (1) concentration, the ability of the mind to stay steady on an object without wavering (2) the cultivation of insight. It means to seek the process of things and the nature of dharma.

48. **The Law of Karmic Excess.** It says that karma incurred in one incarnation can be too overwhelmingly harmonious or disharmonious that to have it all return in one lifetime would put

you out of balance, therefore it is dispersed or worked out in more than one incarnation.

49. **The Law of Release.** It advises you to let go of anything that is no longer useful and purposeful without regrets and resentment. This includes such things as books, philosophy, clothing, beliefs, lifestyle, etc. The pleasure should be in the moment of experience and when it's no longer useful, let go to free yourself to start another learning experience without being bound by the old.

50. **The Law of Ritual.** It says that any act performed repeatedly with specific intent becomes a rite. Each time a ritual is repeated, its power is enhanced in three ways. First, by focusing on the intent, the performer intensifies the power of his mind to control reality. Second, the performer gets permission from his guides and those on the other side to assist him in the desired manifestation. Third, each performance of the rite draws upon the energy of all who have used the rite throughout all time.

You probably need to take a break after reading all these laws. It's okay. It can be overwhelming, especially if you are new to them. The next topic is not as intense as the last but it's also good and I think, you will also find it fascinating.

Heart vs. Brain

Who do you think is smarter, your heart or your brain? Who should you listen to? Are you like me, someone, who used a spreadsheet to figure out the pros and cons before making a decision, or do you just go with your gut without doing any analysis? Our intuition tells us what to do, but we ignore it, then we fail, and then we do it all over again, however many times it takes until we finally get it. I am stubborn so it takes me a while to finally get things. If I had only listened to my gut, I would've avoided a lot of problems. We learn from our mistakes and eventually, we can trust our gut and never doubt it, even if the analysis says differently.

I found this article from Team Soul about heart and brain and it's called: "Listen to your heart, your brain is stupid." To all my analytical readers, pay attention to this as it explains why you should always follow your heart:

"Follow your heart, your brain is stupid. Pay close attention to your feelings. No matter how good something looks, if it doesn't feel right, walk away. If it doesn't feel right, chances are it is not right.

You see your heart is much wiser than your brain. Most people, when faced with a difficult decision, use their brains. Most people believe their intelligence comes from their brain but that is not the case. You see, your heart is the most powerful intelligence in your body. Your heart is the intelligence that came before your brain. Most people don't know that. Yes, your heart started beating before your brain existed. So, the intelligence that created your body and your brain is your heart. We form an emotional brain long before we form a rational one and a beating heart before either. Research shows the heart has 60 times the energy coming out of it as the brain does. Now you can understand how your heart dramatically impacts how your brain works, not the other way around. You can't trust your brain 100% of the time. Your brain wants to keep you safe from all possible forms of pain; your heart wants to take you where you need to go. Living inside your head is not only dangerous, it is reckless.

As Tony Robbins says, "When you're in your head, you're dead". You're dead to the wonder of this world. You're dead to the beauty of this world. You're dead to the clarity of decision making and true peace and clarity that comes from following your heart. To get in touch with your feelings, your heart is a means to unlock all your true potential, peace, and clarity. Your heart knows the way. Follow your gut. Follow your intuition. If you feel like it's right, follow that feeling. Get out of your head, and into your heart. Intuition, following your heart, or acting on a sudden inspiration, has such a negative connotation in society. We are expected to think with our heads and be "practical", but being practical or logical will never lead to true fulfillment or happiness. You can only get that when you live fully, as your authentic self, and follow your heart, even if that doesn't suit those around you.

Jim Carrey said, "So many of us choose our path out of fear, disguised as practicality." As a society, we are so conditioned to conform to 'society standards', which discourages us from following our intuition, from following our hearts. We take the 'practical road' because it is safe, less risky. But when we suppress the desire to act on divine inspiration, we build up tension so great in our soul that we begin to experience lower states of emotion, including depression, anxiety, and disappointment. We miss our path. And for what? So that we can feel "safe"? So that we can have predictability? Sure, predictability and safety have their benefits. But if your heart calls and you choose to ignore it, the consequences may far outweigh the benefits. Your heart will lead you to your authentic self".

Consider someone who is being pressured within a family to join the "family business" to do what generation after generation in his family has done. Is he going to follow his intuition to seek out other avenues, knowing he will be "letting the family down"? Or is he going to suppress his desire to follow a passion? When feeling compelled, yet scared, to take the road unpaved (or "unapproved"), ask yourself the tough questions and be honest with yourself, "Is there some other purpose for me in this life, other than meeting other people's needs and doing what is "expected" of me? Am I more concerned with how others view me, rather than my own happiness? Would doing what is considered normal, or compliant, in this situation cause me to have feelings of fatigue and depression? Am I suppressing my true desires? What will the effects of long-term suppression be, versus the effects of short-term "Acceptance" by friends, family, and society?"

Each of us is gifted with talents and skills which can be identified by looking at the things we are passionate about and inspired to do. By suppressing and turning away from these passions and impulses, we are denying the divine access to powerful creation that exists inside all of us. We are all here for a purpose, and that purpose sometimes does not, at least initially, look so practical. It must be felt, within the heart. You always have the answers inside you. Everything you need is inside you. Just follow your heart, and don't confuse the voices in your head, and around you with the guidance of your much wiser, more powerful heart. Follow your heart... your brain is stupid."

What do you think? Are you now able to trust your heart, or are you going to keep running into the wall until you decide to follow it? It took me four times before I learned. How many times will it take you?

A little over two years ago I finally decided to follow my heart, and it's the best decision I ever made. I did not allow fear of the uncertainty get in the way of my big goals. I was focused on loving myself, gave back to others, got rid of a lot of impurities of the mind, remained in positive vibration so that I could allow people and events to show up in my life to help me accomplish my life's purpose. It took the consistent practice of the mind, but I finally got it. Are you happy with your current situation? If not, what are you going to do to change it? Put this as your action item in the back of this book.

Before you move on to the next chapter, commit to getting rid of any of your limiting beliefs. Change your mindset about money and be open-minded and receptive to what I'm sharing with you. I take it that you are reading this book because you still haven't gotten the result that you're looking for, right? Perhaps you just need to clear your negative programming, but your ego is getting in the way or your intellectual mind cannot rationalize this at all. I'm always a believer that "If there's a will, there's a way." Have a strong will and determination to shift your mindset. Hit the reset button.

Unfortunately, financial success will not happen on its own. You have to carefully plan for it. You need to lay down the proper foundation to secure your future and be able to deal with any financial challenges effectively.

You will need to create a strategy to build, manage, and preserve your wealth. To accomplish this, you will need to look at your current financial situation in detail, determine financial objectives, and develop a plan to bridge the gap from where you are now to where you want to be in the future.

CHAPTER 2
CLEAR GOALS

Your Desires

What are your short-term and long-term financial goals? Is it to be debt-free? Is it to fund kid's college? Is it to retire early? Is it to build generational wealth? You must be very clear on what you want to achieve otherwise it will be difficult to stay focused and achieve the desired results. Once you have a clear goal then write it down and create your vision board. One of the courses I took for CPE is Tax and Financial planning, and on there they noted that less than 4% of Americans ever write down their financial goals, yet setting goals is the most important part of financial planning. Without it, there can be no rational basis for action.

I have a very smart friend. He always comes up with creative business ideas. He starts a project, gets a group of people together to work on it, spends a lot of time and money but then doesn't finish it. Then he'll come up with another business idea, spend a lot of time and money and not finish it again. He had done this over and over. One day I asked him if he ever visualized the result of any of the projects he started, and he answered no. And then I asked if he ever took the time to imagine how he would feel after he completes the project, and he said no. I am telling you this story because I want you to understand that whenever you set goals or you start a project, you must have an end result in mind. You have to "visualize and feel" the emotion, the excitement, and happiness as if you already achieved it. That is the fastest way you can manifest your desire. I don't need to convince you. You simply need to go back to the last chapter and understand the Law of Manifestation, the Law of Belief, and the Law of Attraction.

I'll give you another story to show you that this "visualize and feel" strategy works in whatever goals you set. When I decided to take Accounting as my undergraduate degree, I knew that I had to be a CPA because I wanted designations after my name. That was my clear goal. Then I would visualize writing "CPA" after my name, and I would try to feel what it would be like to have that title for the rest of my life. This is what you have to do with your desired outcome/goals, "visualize and feel" and take necessary action towards your goal. Back in 90's the CPA exam was taken in person and the test was manual. It lasted 2 ½ days (19.5 total hours), and we had to sit for all 5 exams at once. Now the test is taken online and it's one exam at a time so it's a lot easier. Back then, you had to pass two of the five sections.

Any score below 50% on the failed sections and you had to take all 5 sections again. Unfortunately, I didn't study, so even though I passed two sections, I ran out of time, which resulted in a score of less than 50% in a third section. I took a break after this first try. On my second attempt, I didn't go back to Becker's Review. Instead, I bought a whole new review series. If you stack them together it's probably about 10 – 12 inches worth of materials to learn. I did a self-study because I was working full time at PricewaterhouseCoopers and I wanted to study at my own time and not spend time traveling to/from Becker's review class. Back then, there was no such thing as an online review course. On my second exam attempt, I studied, so on the third exam, I only had to take the sections I didn't pass. I'm sharing this story to illustrate that when you have a burning desire to achieve something, you will get it because you won't quit. You'll continue to persevere until you reach your goal. So, have a clear goal in mind, have a burning desire to achieve your goal, "visualize and feel" as if the result is already here, and you're celebrating already.

In one of Bob Proctor's speeches, he said, "The desire alters the vibration, the vibration changes the action, the action sets up an attraction, and that's what changes the result." Going back to my example, my desire to be a CPA put me in a vibration that made me act on that desire and in turn gave me the desired result. If you want to achieve results, you have to be clear about your goal and you must have an amount in mind. Whatever your goal amount is, add another zero at the end. For example, if you want to be a 7-figure earner, add another zero, and aim for 8-figure earnings. Don't be afraid to think big. You must believe that you can achieve it. Do not allow self-doubt or negative self-talk.

Generational Values and Differences

This topic, I think you will find interesting. I think it's important that we have a good understanding of how each generation's upbringing, core values, and challenges are so that we can understand how they view life and money. If you are a parent, teacher, or life coach this will help you with your approach when helping your children or your clients make important decisions.

According to Pew Research, as of today, we have seven different generations: G.I.(1901–1927), Silent (1928 – 1945), Boomer (1946 – 1964), Gen X (1965 – 1980), Gen Y/Millennials (1981 – 1996), Gen Z/Digital Native (1997 – 2012), and Gen Alpha (anyone born after 2013). As of July 1, 2019, Millennials have surpassed Baby Boomers as the United States' largest living adult generation.

G.I. and Silent generation

They say that the G.I. generation is the greatest generation because they saved the world in World War II and then build a great nation in the years when they lead the country in the 50s–70s. The Silent generation grew up during the Great Depression and World War II and they believe that you had to earn your way through life by hard work and long hours. They believe that career advancement should be the result of experience, tenure, proven productivity, and results. They want comfort and financial security. They are patriotic, have traditional family values, and are loyal employees.

Boomer generation

World War II ended in 1945 so American troops came home all at once, reunited with their loved ones, got married, and suddenly the wedding industry was a $3 Billion industry. Nine months later, there was a baby boom, the Boomers. They grew up experiencing strong families, safe neighborhoods, communities were connected, jobs were plentiful and stable, moms were able to be stay-at-home moms if they wished. There was a lot of security and stability. They grew up in such love and hope that they grew optimism and idealism. They are the first generation who enjoyed empowerment during their youth. They are honorable, patriotic, compassionate, ethical, bold, fearless, and triumphant, but they challenged social structure, social norms, and were the source of the civil rights movement and second-wave feminism. They struggled with marriage, and the divorce rate skyrocketed. They also struggled with parenting.

Gen X generations

Generation X also is known as Gen X, or the latchkey generation comprises 21% of the US population which makes them smaller than other generations. This generation grew up seeing an increase in their family's household income due to civil rights and second-wave feminism. Though they enjoyed more household income growing up, they endured the most difficult childhood in American history as their parents divorced. Career moms became widespread. They experienced having to move homes because their parents' jobs relocated and they got separated from a place where they were familiar and felt safe. This generation saw their political and Christian leaders fall in disgrace, and the corporate leaders dismantle the great American middle class. The middle-class income dropped for the first time since World War II. The rich got richer and the blue-collar workers got trampled. There were massive layoffs that affected the parents of Gen X. Because of these experiences, the core values of Gen X are independent, entrepreneurial, self-reliant, individualistic, results-oriented, cynical, distrustful, and self-focused. This is my generation, but my family immigrated to the U.S. from the Philippines in the 80s, so I may not have all the Gen X qualities as described in this generation research. Gen X generation became the family-first generation where they seek work-life balance and have the mentality that they always must be there for their children. They are the generation who rebuilt the American family unit and because of this, they became helicopter parents to their Millennial/Gen Z children as they tried to protect them from any setbacks. In my case, I would agree and disagree with this statement. As a single parent raising my one and only child, I was protective of my son. I wanted the best for him, of course, but trained him to be independent because I wanted to make sure he would be fine just in case something happened to me. Although, it wasn't easy raising him alone while working in public accounting and working crazy hours, I managed. This is probably why it's easy for me to set a goal and things get done because of my time management skills which a lot of people find difficult.

Millennial generations

According to research, Millennial children tend to seek their parents' advice for important decisions. This generations' core values are optimistic, enthusiastic, outgoing, respectful of their elder's wisdom, and have close relationships with their parents. Because this generation has access to information easily, they tend to be impatient, have short attention spans; they crave variety and change. They are so tech addicts that it diminished their soft skills. They are the generation who experienced severe financial stress due to things that happened when they were just getting out of college and found themselves unemployed in 2010.

The Great Recession has split the millennials into two distinct groups, those who took the greatest hit from the recession and dealt with a tough job market and those who experienced the recovery period and entered a better job market. The older millennials are still recovering from the recession while the younger millennials have more time to plan financially. Since the younger millennials didn't experience the financial crisis directly, they were able to observe it and learn what to do and what not to do. They are more aware of the risk of a bad economy. They are more practical when it comes to money, working hard to catch up financially, and prioritize financial success before getting married. Millennials in the graduating class of 2018 have an average student loan debt of $29K and this is hindering their ability to save.

Gen Z generations

According to Business Insider Intelligence, Generation Z, also known as iGen or centennials, are the youngest, and largest generation in American history. They grew up with technology, the internet, and social media, which at times causes them to be stereotyped as tech-addicted, anti-social, or "social justice warriors." The average Gen Z got their first smartphone just before turning 12 years old. They communicate through social media and texts and spend as much time on their phones as older generations do watching TV. They will soon become the most pivotal generation in the future of retail, and many will have huge spending power by 2026.

Generation Alpha

The youngest generation is Generation Alpha, and they are set to be the most transformative generation yet. They haven't just grown up with technology, they've been completely immersed in it since birth. They don't consider technologies to be tools but rather as deeply integrated parts of everyday life.

What generation are you and can you relate to this research? Hopefully, this will help you gain a better understanding of the people you deal with because when you understand the way people are, you'll be more compassionate to others. So far, I haven't taught you anything about finance, money, or wealth, but there's a reason why I wrote this book this way. The financial concepts and strategies that I will be sharing may not help you unless mindset is in the right place. I want to make sure that you identify and become aware of any negative programming you have about money so that you can release it. I want to make sure you know that you have the power to hit the reset button and start over again no matter what stage you are in your financial life. I want to make sure you understand that it's important to reward yourself and celebrate the little and big accomplishments you've achieved towards your goal as this helps you stay motivated. I want to make sure you understand that emotional intelligence is as important as your intellectual intelligence. I want to make sure you understand the Universal Laws so you can use them to your advantage and lastly, I want to make sure that you'll learn to follow your heart and to trust your intuition because it's always right.

Know the Fundamentals

Whatever your financial goals may be, you must understand the basics of accounting and finance. Do you know how important your credit score is?

Do you know how to build a strong financial foundation as you would build a strong house? Do you understand how Rule 72 can affect your financial goal immensely? Have you created or updated your financial statements recently? Are you managing your debt properly? We're going to cover these topics in this chapter. Ready?

The first thing I want to talk about is Credit Score because it is very important that you understand the implication of your score and also educate your family so they don't make a financial decision that will adversely impact their life. I suggest you get a pen and pad or use the notes in the back of this book so you can write down action items that may come to mind when you are reading so you can come back to them later.

Credit Score

Keeping a good credit score is particularly important. Your score can affect the way people view you and the way you look at yourself. According to Experian, there are many different types of credit scores, FICO and VantageScore are the two common types. VantageScore is commonly used by lenders and it was developed by the three major credit bureaus (Experian, Equifax, and TransUnion). The latest VantageScore 3.0 model uses a range between 300 to 850.

RATING	CREDIT SCORE	IMPACT
Very Poor	300 – 499	Applicants will not likely be approved for credit
Poor	500 – 600	Applicants may be approved for some credit, though rates may be unfavorable and with conditions such as larger down payment amounts
Fair	601 – 660	Applicants may be approved for credit but likely not at competitive rates
Good	661 – 780	Applicants likely to be approved for credit at competitive rates
Excellent	781 – 850	Applicants most likely to receive the best rate and most favorable terms on credit accounts

As you can see from the above table, your credit score will impact the rate the lender will offer you, and not only that, depending on the job you're applying for, employers can check your credit score. It can be used in deciding whether to hire you or not. It's so easy to lose points and so difficult to gain them back. According to Credit Karma, the things that can highly impact your credit score are, payment history, credit card utilization, and any derogatory marks. Other markers such as credit age, total accounts, and hard inquiries have medium/low impact.

Regarding your payment history, a single 30 or 60 day missed payment is easier to recover from, but it can hurt your score significantly. A 90-day missed payment is more damaging and could disqualify you from certain loans. You must stay mindful of your due dates. I suggest that you set up an auto payment to pay your credit card when due. If you cannot pay your balance off, at least set it up so that when it's due, the minimum payment is paid which avoids late payment charges. If you are consistently paying your credit card payment on time and for whatever reason, you missed a payment, call the credit card company and request to have the fee waived. If you have a good track record, they will waive it for you. Before you call, make sure you put on a smile and ask nicely. Being nice and kind always go a long way.

Regarding your credit card utilization, try to stay under 30%. If you can stay under 10% that's even better. The credit utilization ratio is calculated by taking your credit card balance and divide it by the total credit limit amount.

Regarding derogatory marks, if you have collection notices or public records, they can stay on your report for 7-10 years. If you have a collection record that is not accurate, you should dispute it. Public records such as tax liens, civil judgments, and bankruptcies are harder to remove.

Regarding credit age, lenders like to see that you have experience using credit responsibly, so don't close your oldest credit card because it's what gives you long credit history. Note though that sometimes, credit card companies will close an old account that you don't use so remember to use it once in a while to prevent the company from closing the account which can potentially drop your credit score. This happened to me. I had one that has a $20K limit it closed because of non-usage. This can also affect your utilization rate so be mindful.

Regarding total accounts, lenders like to see that you've used a variety of accounts responsibly so having different account types (credit cards, car loans, home loans) can help your credit.

Regarding hard inquiries, they have a low impact when compared to other items that affect your credit. Hard inquiries from things like credit applications can stay on your report for up to 2 years, but their effects fade over time. If you are planning to get a big loan such as a mortgage loan, plan, and minimize your hard inquiries to at least 9 to 12 months before trying to get a loan. Soft inquiries do not impact your credit score. Soft inquiries occur when you check your credit report, use credit monitoring services, when inquiries are made by companies offering promotional offers of credit, or your lender conducts a periodic review of your accounts.

Do you have Credit Karma online account or app on your phone? If not, I suggest you upload it on your phone or register online so you're able to track your score. Just don't get obsessed by checking it all the time because it will fluctuate a few points here and there. Also, if you go to *www.annualcreditreport.com*, you can request a free report from each of the three credit reporting companies (Transunion, Equifax, and Experian). It's a good idea to request it every 12 months so you'll have an opportunity to review and correct any error which, as you now know, can significantly affect you. I also suggest that you call the three credit bureaus and freeze your credit. If you don't have good credit, it's okay. As I suggested in the last chapter, you can always press the reset button and start over again. Always be kind to yourself. Forget about the mistakes made and start focusing on building a positive credit history. How will you accomplish that? What if you haven't built your credit yet?

According to Experian, you can open a credit card account. If you think you are not going to get approved, then get a secured credit card. A secured credit card is tied to your savings account, and the limit on the card is usually the amount in the account or a percentage of it. Keep your balance low and pay it on time. Note though that not all lenders report secured credit cards to the credit bureaus, but the lender may be willing to convert the account to a traditional credit card after a period of time. I suggest that you ask this question before deciding whether to open a secured credit card account.

Other ways to help build credit is to ask someone with established credit to co-sign a loan for you, open a joint credit card account or add you as an authorized user. I did this for my son when he went to college, and it helped him establish his credit. Once his credit was established, I removed his name as an authorized user. Other ways to build credit are, to request a credit limit increase, pay your student loan diligently, take out an auto installment loan, obtain a secured loan and ask your landlord and utility company to report your positive payment history to the credit bureaus.

These are the common mistakes that you should avoid such as, not knowing how to manage debt, not knowing your debt-to-income ratio, not having a budget, not understanding how much you can afford, not doing comparison shopping to find the lowest available interest rates on your installment loans, failing to protect yourself from fraud, and applying for multiple credit cards in a short amount of time.

Four Life Stages

Just like building a house, your financial house must also be built with a strong foundation and you must build it from the ground up. There are four financial life stages: Protection, Accumulation, Distribution, and Legacy. The protection stage is the stage when you protect your family's lifestyle, meet your family's growing needs, and start a savings plan. The accumulation stage is the stage when you continue to grow your wealth, plan for your retirement, and protect your savings and investments. The distribution stage is the stage when you enjoy your retirement; it's when you continue to generate income, and when you protect your retirement plan. The legacy stage is the stage when you preserve your estate. It's when you plan how your wealth will be transferred. Now, that you understand the different financial stages, which stage are you in currently?

Four Types of Planning

Your needs vary as you go through different life stages. The four different types of planning are Defensive, Offensive, Aggressive, and Progressive. **Defensive planning** is when you plan for an unexpected death and/or disability. The goal here is to protect your loved ones, what you own, what you owe, and what you earn. If you are an employee, your salary stops upon death. If you become disabled, depending on your employee benefits, you may or may not receive a portion of your salary. Who will pay for your personal and/or household expenses then? You want to make sure you meticulously plan for this type of circumstance. You are lucky if your employer provides life insurance through a group plan. This will help your family in case of your death but what if that runs out? Employee life insurance coverage is usually between 2 to 4 times the annual salary. How much is your coverage? Would that be sufficient? What if you don't have life insurance through work? In a later chapter, you will learn about the different types of financial products.

The second type of planning is **Offensive planning**. This is when you plan for major purchases such as a house. This is also when you plan for emergencies, children's college education, and retirement. The third planning is **Aggressive planning**.

This is when you try to overpower inflation. This is when you maximize your qualified plan contributions and utilize diversification strategies to reduce your risk. The fourth and final planning is **Progressive planning**. This is when you plan on how to transfer assets you accumulated in the most tax-efficient manner. This is also when the conversation about charitable giving, estate preservation, and business continuity planning happens.

Where are you in your planning? Make sure you seek professional's advice so that you may be guided properly, and also avoid costly mistakes. Tax rules are complex, and change all the time, so you have to continuously review your plan to make sure it is the most tax-efficient. This is why as a CPA, I have to maintain at least 40 hours of continuing professional education (CPE) credits each year.

Cash Flow Quadrants

The authors of "Rich Dad, Poor Dad," Robert Kiyosaki and Sharon Lechter, described four different types of people by their types of income. The people on the left side of the quadrant are: Employees (E) and Self Employed (S). E's have jobs while S's own jobs. These people earn a Linear Income. This is a type of income where you trade time for money. These people will never be financially independent because when they stop working due to illness, disability, unemployment, or retirement, their income will stop too.

The people on the right side of the quadrant are Business Owners (B) and Investors (I). These people earn Residual Income. This is a type of income that keeps coming from the work they have already done. Their income is not dependent on their presence. B's leverage is the people they hire while I's leverage makes money work for them.

During an economic downturn, E's and S's usually suffer the most because jobs become scarce and the cost of living goes up. B's and I's on the other hand get richer because they have the cash to buy the best assets at rock bottom price and when the economy picks up, the assets they invested in will pay dividends at the lowest tax rates. They do well in both down and up markets.

Now you've seen the different types of people in the cash flow quadrants, who do you think pays less in income tax, the E's/S's or the B's/I's? The answer is, the B's and the I's because they use strategies to mitigate the one thing they cannot control, income tax rates. You don't have to wait until you're on the right side of the quadrant to take advantage of this no matter where you are in your financial life stage. If you are an E, ask yourself what you're passionate about and create a business utilizing your passion. The reason why I say this is because, when you're passionate about something, you don't mind doing it. Your business wouldn't feel like another job that you hate.

This explains why the rich get richer and the poor get poorer. Rich people use the knowledge they learn and use it to their advantage by making wise financial decisions.

Which side are you in the quadrant? Make every effort to get on the right-hand side of the quadrant.

The IRS provides publications about various topics that are easy to read, not like the Internal Revenue Code, so if you want to read about, "Starting a Business and Keeping Records", you can look at Publication 583. If you want to learn about Business Expenses, see Publication 535, for "Business Use of Home," see Publication 587. This is the link if you want to see the full list: https://www.irs.gov/publications

Three Primary Financial Statements

Have you ever created your personal financial statement? Unless a lender or an investor requested this from you, it's likely that you probably have not prepared this. I want to go over three personal financial statements that are typically used (i.e. **Statement of Cash Flows**, **Income Statement**, and **Balance Sheet**). I'll explain what they are, what they're for, and why you should prepare them.

The Intermediate Accounting textbook defines Statement of Cash Flow as, "one of the primary financial statement which reports the cash receipts, cash payments, and net change in cash resulting from the operating, investing, and financing activities of an enterprise during a period in a format that reconciles the beginning and ending cash balances." According to Financial Accounting Standards Board (FASB), the information provided in this statement of cash flows, if used with related disclosures and information in other financial statements, should help investors and creditors to assess the enterprise's ability to generate positive future net cash flows, and meet its obligations. If you have Excel, you can prepare this statement from scratch or use a template that's provided called "Small Business Cash Flow Forecast" and simply modify it to accommodate your personal cash flow information.

The Intermediate Accounting textbook defines an Income Statement as, "the report that measures the success of enterprise operation for a given time.

The business and investment community uses this report to determine investment value, creditworthiness, and income success". The Income Statement reports income and expenses over a period of time. It could be for a certain month, quarter, or year.

Examples of income are the salaries, wages, commissions, tips, bonuses you received from your employer, interest income from your bank, or people you loan money to, dividend income from your ownership of a business, active or passive income from your pass-through entities (LLC or S-Corp), rental income from your assets which you are leasing, equipment or real property, whether it's a land, residential or commercial buildings. Examples of expenses are your utilities, food, clothing, rent, auto/home/life/health insurance, telephone, and internet. The formula for Net Income is, (Total Income + Gains from the sale of assets) – (Total Expenses + Losses from the sale of assets). If you have Excel, you can prepare this from scratch or use a template that's provided called "Profit and Loss Statement" or "Income Statement." To figure out your annual net profit amount or net income, you would take the sum of all your income for the year and then deduct all your expenses for the year. There's a blank Income Statement sample provided in the Appendix. Your income statement will look similar. It will have the revenue and expenses portion but not the cost of goods sold. Pause for a moment and create your income statement before you move on.

The Intermediate Accounting textbook defines a Balance Sheet as, "the report which provides information about the nature and amounts of investments in enterprise resources, obligations on enterprise creditors, and the owner's equity in net enterprise resources." Basically, it reports your assets, liabilities, and your equity at a specific date. Its purpose is to show your net worth at a given time. Lenders and investors use the balance sheet to decide whether to extend more credit while they use the income statement to decide whether or not you are making enough to pay for your liabilities. The Balance Sheet formula is Assets = Liabilities + Equity. This means you have to pay for everything you own (Assets) by either taking out a loan (Liability) or by contributing capital (Equity). If you have Excel, you can prepare this from scratch or use a template that's provided called "Balance Sheet." There's a blank Net Worth Balance Sheet sample provided in the Appendix. Pause for a moment and create your personal balance sheet before you move on.

Asset as defined by Kiyosaki

Robert Kiyosaki defines Assets as items that put money in your pocket while Liabilities cost you money. Examples of Assets are your cash, cash equivalents (CD's, checking, savings, money market), investments (treasury bills, stocks, bonds, real properties, intangible properties), furniture, equipment, artwork, and jewelry). Examples of Liabilities are student loans, mortgage debt, car notes, and other secured/unsecured loans. Some people think that the house they live in is an asset, some think it is a liability. We said earlier that an asset puts money in your pocket so is your house putting money in your pocket? If your house is a duplex where you live on one side of the house and the other side is rented, then your house is an asset because it's putting money in your pocket by getting rental income every month. The difference between the market value of your home and what your balance is in your mortgage note is the equity in your home. If you add all your assets and deduct all of your liabilities, the difference is your equity. So, what is your equity?

If you want to build wealth, you need to understand the different types of assets and find a way to acquire them. If you are an employee, think about a business that you can start on the side. Having a business allows you to write off a lot of expenses that are not tax-deductible as an employee. You can be an insurance agent. You can be a real estate agent. You can sell services or products online. Find what you enjoy doing and what you are passionate about and leverage your passion and talent. Doing so will put more money in your pocket which will eventually help you to acquire more assets. Another way to acquire assets is by leveraging other people's money. Therefore it's important who you surround yourself with. With proper connections, you'd be able to find the people and resources you need to achieve your goals faster.

Sharon Lechter's Success Formula

In Sharon Lechter's books, her private Facebook group, and her webinars she taught the Formula for Success. The formula is $((P+T) \times A \times A) + F$ which translates to: ((Passion + Talent) x Association x Action + Faith. As you can see here, the power of association and having your mastermind group is especially important in your success. When you decide to make some changes in your life for the better, you might have to let go of some of the people in your life. It can be temporary; it can be permanent.

Hopefully, you can better yourself and go back to those people and teach them what you learned. Please note that more detailed information about financial statements can be found in the General Securities chapter.

Budgeting

Now that you understand the three primary financial statements, budgeting is the next topic I want you to learn because this is a necessary activity in your wealth-building program and besides, the only way for you not to go beyond your means is by having a budget. Create a budget that you are willing to commit to every month and make sure, it's not excessively strict. If you have Excel, you will find a budget template called "Personal Monthly Budget" and "Household monthly Budget." By going through this exercise, it will not only help you with planning, but this will also serve as a control system whereas you can contain your expenses and develop discretionary income.

There are five basic budget rules. Rule no. 1 is to try to control your expenses so they don't exceed 60% of your gross income. If you're not quite there yet, it's okay, just make sure you review your expenses and see where you can make some changes or better yet, find a way to make more money by starting a part-time business. You will hear me say this to you all the time because I want you to be a business owner. This is the only way for you to get ahead. Rule no. 2, by having effective tax planning you can keep your income tax at 20% or less of your gross income. If you're an employee, you can complete Form W-4 to adjust your taxes withheld. Rule no. 3 is to save 10% of your gross income. The purpose is so that you accumulate funds to acquire investments thereby building wealth. Rule no. 4 is, spend 10% of your income on continuing practical education that motivates you to act, take risks, and learn financial principles. Outlays for educational seminars, materials, publications, and professional services can result in savings many times over. These expenses should be considered as investments that will produce future returns. Rule no. 5 is that 50% of any benefit or "found" money such as inheritances, tax refunds, gifts, salary raises, etc. should go to savings and the other 50% can be blown on lifestyle without feelings of guilt.

Bank Reconciliation

Do you reconcile your bank account every month? Reconciling your bank account every month is particularly important because you need to make sure that what the bank is recording is the same as what you are recording in your internal financial record. When performing this exercise, you may find inaccurate charges, late fees, penalties, and deposits in your internal record but not in the bank record and vice versa. If you are not reconciling, your internal record may not be accurate, and you may think you have more money available in your account than you do. Checks and withdrawals may have cleared the bank that you neglected to record resulting in inaccuracies.

If this happens you may incur overdraft charges, so pay attention to both your bank and your internal records. If you have Excel, you can use a template that is provided called "Monthly Bank Reconciliation."

Debt Management

Why is it important to manage your debt? It's important because debt can get out of hand. When you're not controlling your debt, it's controlling you. You need to have a plan on how you will pay off all your debts. If you haven't already, you should create a summary of all your debts and show lender/creditor/investor information, interest rates, and balance amounts. Doing this will help you organize, prioritize, and create a plan to pay them off. You can sort your debts by balance amounts or by interest rates. Some teach that you should focus on paying off small balances first, regardless of the interest rate while others prioritize paying off the high-interest rate debts first. Dave Ramsey teaches the former. The method is called, debt snowball method where you list your debts from smallest to largest.

You make minimum payments on all your debts except the one that has the smallest balance. You pay as much as possible on your smallest debt and then repeat this until each debt is paid in full. In Excel, you will find a template called Credit Card Payoff Calculator which shows the effect of paying a minimum payment versus a proposed monthly payment (see appendix). It shows the months and the total interest you will pay if you pay a minimum payment versus your proposed payment. Whichever method you are comfortable with, the goal is the same, to be debt-free so decide which method, put it into place, and commit not to add any more debt.

Some people will teach you not to carry credit cards, but if you are disciplined enough then go ahead and carry one, just as long as you pay it off when it becomes due. There are benefits to carrying one. If you're like me and love to travel, you earn miles that apply to hotels and airfare. There was one year when I had a lot of mileage and used some of them to purchase gift cards and give them away during the holidays. That's a gift that didn't have to come out of your pocket.

Another debt reduction strategy you can use is your mortgage prepayment. If you received unexpected money, or you have extra cash, you can send that to your lender and have them apply it to your mortgage principal. Later you will learn the effect of simple and compounding interest.

Retirement Plan Types

There are various types of Retirement plans and each of them has its own rules and tax implications so make sure you understand them to so you can assess whether your existing plan is good. You may want to use multiple plans for tax diversification. Below are some of the common plans.

Traditional IRA (Individual Retirement Arrangements). You can contribute to this plan if you (or your spouse if filing jointly) have taxable compensation. You can deduct your contribution from your tax return if you qualify. The contribution limit for 2020 is $6K ($7K if you're age 50 and older). There is a Required Minimum Distribution (RMD) when you turn age 72 (per the current tax rule). Any deductible contributions and earnings you withdraw or that are distributed from this plan are taxable. There is a 10% early withdrawal penalty if you are not 59 ½ or older at the time of withdrawal.

ROTH IRA. You can contribute to this plan if you (or your spouse if filing jointly) have taxable compensation and modified adjusted gross income is below certain amounts. You cannot deduct your contribution from your tax return. The contribution limit for 2020 is $6K ($7K if you're age 50 and older). There is no RMD in this plan unless you are not the original owner.

There is no tax on the qualified distribution but there is a 10% early withdrawal penalty if you are not 59 ½ or older at the time of withdrawal.

401(k) Plan. This plan allows employees to contribute a portion of their wages to individual accounts. Elective salary deferrals are excluded from the employee's taxable income. Employers can contribute to employees' accounts. Distributions and earnings are included in taxable income at retirement. The limit on employee elective deferrals is $19,500 in 2020.

403(b) Plan. This plan is also called a tax-sheltered annuity or TSA plan. This is a retirement plan offered by public schools and certain 501(c)(3) tax-exempt organizations. Employees save for retirement by contributing to individual accounts. Employers can also contribute to employees' accounts. Just as with a 401(k) plan, this plan allows employees to defer some of their salaries into individual accounts. The most an employee can contribute to this plan is $19,500 in 2020. If permitted by the plan, employees who are age 50 or over at the end of the calendar year can also make <u>catch-up contributions</u> of $6,500 in 2020. The deferred salary is generally not subject to federal or state income tax until it's distributed otherwise, there will be a possible <u>10% penalty</u> if under age 59-1/2.

457(b) Plan. The organization must be a state or local government or a tax-exempt organization under IRC 501(c) to have this plan. Employers or employees through salary reductions contribute up to $19,500 in 2020. The contributions are tax-deferred and earnings on the retirement money are also tax-deferred.

SEP IRA Plan. Simplified Employee Pension Plan allows employers to contribute to traditional IRAs set up for employees. A business of any size, even self-employed, can establish this plan. This plan does not have the start-up and operating costs of a conventional retirement plan and allows contributions of up to 25% of each employee's pay. There is no filing requirement for the employer and the employer can contribute. An employee is always 100% vested in all of the money in the plan.

SIMPLE IRA Plan. Savings Incentive Match Plan for Employees allows employees and employers to contribute to traditional IRAs set up for employees. It is ideally suited as a start-up retirement savings plan for small employers (100 or fewer) not currently sponsoring a retirement plan. The employer cannot have any other retirement plan. There is no filing requirement for the employer. The employer is required to contribute each year by either matching contribution up to 3% of compensation or 2% nonelective contribution for each eligible employee. Employees may elect to contribute and are always 100% vested in all of the money in the plan.

If you want to learn more about retirement plans, you may visit the IRS website and look for the following Publications 560, 571, 575, 590, and 939.

See appendix for Retirement Planning Tax Efficiency Check-up and Questionnaire.

Your Clear Goal

Before you move on to the next chapter, pause for a minute, and look at the notes you took. Are there action items that you need to address right away? If so, put a date next to them and make sure you put them in your calendar. The next two chapters are technical materials. While reading, you will come across concepts that may help you with your current plan. When you do, do not just keep reading, you need to take notes because you will not remember. Have a clear goal in mind because when you do, it's easier to identify what steps you need to take towards that goal.

CHAPTER 3
BASIC TAX AND FINANCIAL CONCEPTS

In this chapter, you will be introduced to concepts that you may or may not already know. Nonetheless, these are important concepts that will help you develop a plan or improve your current plan to achieve your goals faster.

Rule of 72

Have you heard of Rule of 72 before? It's okay if you haven't but it's important that to understand what this is as it affects your money. The banks don't want you to know this rule and you will understand why later. Rule of 72 is a term used to describe a method that calculates the number of years it takes to double an investment's value at a given rate of return. The genius behind this formula is Albert Einstein.

If you are lucky, you will find a rate of return of over 1% in your savings bank, but let's use 1% in our example to keep the math simple. If you take 72 and divide it by the rate of 1, it will take 72 years to double your money. So, if you have 10K in the bank earning that rate, you will have 20K in 72 years. This example is important so that you don't put your money into vehicles that won't work for you.

Now let's use the Rule of 72 on debts. Let's just say that you have a credit card balance of $15K, and since you have good credit, they offer you an interest rate of 19%. If you take 72 and divide it by 19, it will take 3.78 years to double your balance which means your credit card's new balance will be 30K in just less than 4 years. Don't these two examples make you mad? Have you ever wondered why personal finance is not taught in high school in states yet? By the time you're done reading this book, you will know exactly what you need to do to take control of your finance and to create wealth, but will you do it? I hope so. That's why I am incorporating a contest to be awarded in our annual conference to motivate you, to encourage you, and for you to meet other people at the conference who took action as you did.

Simple interest vs. Compounding Interest

Why should you care whether something is calculated using the simple versus compounding interest method? Well, knowing this basic financial concepts can help you make informed decisions when taking out a loan or investing. The Simple Interest is calculated on the principal or original amount while Compound Interest is calculated on the principal amount and the accumulated interest of the previous periods. Let's consider that you have $50,000 in an investment vehicle earning 6% simple interest in Bank S and another $50,000 in Bank C with a 6% compounding interest annually.

Bank S:

Year	Principal	Interest	Total Interest	Balance
Year 1	50,000	6%	$3,000	53,000
Year 2	50,000	6%	$3,000	56,000
Year 3	50,000	6%	$3,000	59,000
Year 4	50,000	6%	$3,000	62,000
Year 5	50,000	6%	$3,000	65,000

Bank C:

Year	Principal	Interest	Total Interest	Balance
Year 1	50,000	6%	$3,000	53,000.00
Year 2	53,000	6%	$3,180	56,180.00
Year 3	56,180	6%	$3,370.80	59,550.80
Year 4	59,550.80	6%	$3,573.05	63,123.85
Year 5	63,123.85	6%	$3,787.43	66,911.28

As you can see, you will grow your money faster when your money is in an investment vehicle earning interest compounding annually. Now that you learned some of the basic accounting and finance concepts, how to manage your debt better, and how to increase cash flow by finding ways to generate additional income, the next thing I want you to learn is the different component that affects your money.

Wealth Creation

Did anyone take their time to teach you how you create wealth faster? Your Parents? Your Teachers? Your School? I have a feeling they have not. That's why you're reading this book and that's why we have 67% of people worldwide who are not financially literate. Why were we deprived of this knowledge? Are we programmed to not be wealthy? Why? Why? Why? My undergraduate degree is in Accounting, but they didn't teach wealth creation in class. It wasn't until much later when I put things into place. I guess it wasn't my priority at that time because I was busy working for someone while raising my son as a single mom. I didn't pay much attention to this, but I wish I had because we can never get back time. That's why it became my passion and obsession to teach our children. Let me explain the different components that affect your money: Inflation, Rate of Return, Time, and Taxes.

Inflation

Why should you learn what inflation is? Well, if you don't know how this affects your money then you may think that the money in your savings account is growing when it's not.

Inflation is an increase in the level of prices of goods and services that households buy. The most well-known indicator is the Consumer Price Index (CPI), which measures the percentage change in the price of a basket of goods and services consumed by average households. Inflation makes money saved today less valuable tomorrow so when you're building wealth you want to make sure your money is invested in a vehicle that is substantially higher than the inflation rate, otherwise you are losing money every day. For example, if you have your money saved in a savings account or money market account earning less than 1% and the inflation rate is 2%, this means you are not overpowering inflation. You are losing money every day, but you know what? A lot of people keep their money in a savings account, money market, or CD. Why? Because they're not well educated. I'm sure that if they had proper education and understood inflation, that wouldn't be the case at all. A savings account should only be used as deferred investing, not as an investment vehicle. When savings accounts have accumulated sufficiently, they should be used to buy more assets. Assets that will eventually create passive income.

Rate of Return

Do you know how to calculate the rate of return in your investments? The rate of return (ROR) is the percentage increase or decrease over your initial investment. It represents what you have earned or lost on your investment. The formula is: ROR = (new value of investment − old value of investment) x 100% / old value of investment. What do you think is considered a good rate of return? It depends on the individual investor. An investor may settle for a lower ROR to keep the risk minimal while others choose to invest in a higher ROR because their risk tolerance is much higher.

Time

Earlier you learned the power of compounding interest and how it can help you reach your goals faster. Another important component is time. If you are not putting any money away, no matter how insignificant it is, you are losing out. My drive to deliver this book to as many people as possible is because of time. I want people to be educated and put what they learn into action.

If your employer is offering a retirement plan (401k, 403b, SIMPLE IRA, SEP plan) where they match your contribution, make a point to contribute up to that amount. For example, if your employer is matching 100% of your first 5% contribution then try to contribute 5% or higher in the retirement plan.

The Difference Time and Compounding Interest Can Make

Early planning can help you maximize the power of time in reaching your financial goals. The sooner you begin to save for your future financial needs, the more wealth you can accumulate. Although the idea is straightforward and logical, most people fail to recognize the enormous increase in value that can result from beginning to save early.

The best way to demonstrate the power of time is by way of example. Let's look at the different approaches to investing taken by twin sisters, The Finance Doctor, and The Procrastinator.

<u>The Finance Doctor started to save early</u>

Looking to build a large nest egg for her retirement, The Finance Doctor chose to invest $1,000 per year in an Individual Retirement Annuity (an IRA funded by an annuity), starting at age 30.

She continued her payments for 10 years until age 40, earning an average of 6% per year on her investments. At age 40, she stopped contributing to the IRA but, she left her $11,000 of contributions in the account, plus earnings, until retirement at age 65.

The Procrastinator started to save late

The Procrastinator was also a bright lady who saw the need to put money away for her retirement, but since she's a procrastinator, she didn't begin implementing her investment plan until she was age 45. At that point, she began investing $1,000 a year in an IRA. She also averaged a 6% annual return but continued to make $1,000 investments for 20 years until she retired at age 65. Her contributions over the years totaled $20,000.

Given the fact that The Procrastinator contributed $9,000 more than The Finance Doctor, you might expect that The Procrastinator would have a significantly greater total for retirement at age 65 but surprisingly, just the opposite is true. Assuming the tax-deferred IRA of each twin earned 6% a year, the account balance for The Finance Doctor at age 65 would be $68,117, while The Procrastinator would have only $38,993.

Earnings Earn Earnings

The Procrastinator was on the right track. She invested steadily and wisely, earning good returns but she made a big mistake; she got a late start. So, even though she invested almost twice the amount the Finance Doctor did, she had less money to enjoy at retirement. Now, look at her twin's experience. By getting an earlier start, The Finance Doctor benefited from 15 more years of compounded interest. Left to accumulate in her account, the earnings from her early years earned additional returns.

It's Never Too Early for You to Start Saving

Although today's responsibilities may take up most of your time and attention, it's important to consider what you want to accomplish in the future. With a growing family, you may need to buy your first home or one with more space. You may want to launch your own business, which could require heavy start-up expenses. With college tuition on the rise, you may be facing another big expense when your children are ready for higher education. You may need more money to support the lifestyle you want in retirement, which may last 20 or 30 years or more.

Taxes

Currently, we are in a low-income tax environment, and we don't know when this will change but do you think the tax rates will go up or go down? Do you know the highest marginal tax rate in US history? In the years 1944-1945, income above $200K was taxed at 94%. Are you shocked? I was when I first learned this. Can you imagine earning $100K and only being allowed to keep $6K? Could this happen again? This is one moment in history I wouldn't want to repeat.

As of 2020, seven states do not levy personal income tax: Alaska, Florida, Nevada, South Dakota, Texas, Washington, and Wyoming. Living in a state that doesn't tax income can be a major advantage. I relocated from Illinois to Florida in 2006 and saved a lot of money in state income tax and sales tax. The income tax rate also plays an important role when you are trying to figure out whether to invest in pre-tax or post-tax investment vehicles. Some people prefer to pay tax now and not worry about paying it later. Others prefer to take the risk and pay tax later. Later, we will go over the tax implications of paying tax on the seed versus paying tax on the harvest.

Tax Types

Have you ever wondered how many different types of tax imposed on us by the government? Well, there are three different types. The first type is the taxes you pay on what you earn. Examples of this type of tax are individual income taxes, corporate income taxes, payroll taxes, and capital gains taxes. The second type is taxes you pay on what you purchase. Examples of this type of tax are, sales taxes, gross receipts taxes, value-added taxes, and excise taxes. The third type is taxes on what you own. Examples of this type of tax are, property taxes, tangible personal property taxes, estate and inheritance taxes, and wealth taxes. Which one of these taxes do you pay?

How would you like to know ways to reduce your taxes so you can minimize what you pay? Later you will learn different tax strategies you can use as an individual and/or business owner and this is exactly what the business owners (B's) and investors (I's) on the right-hand side of Kiyosaki's cash flow quadrant do. They pay smart people who know the constantly changing and complex tax rules and use the code sections from the Internal Revenue Code to help them structure their business affairs in the most tax-efficient manner.

First type: Tax on what you earn

Individual income taxes or personal income tax is levied on the salaries, wages, investments, or other forms of income an individual earns. This tax is "progressive" which means tax rates increase as the individual taxpayer's income increases. So, if this is the case then, why do the B's and I's from Kiyosaki's cash flow quadrant pay less tax or no tax than the ones on the left side of the quadrant (E's and S's)? They have several businesses where they take tax write-offs. They use various strategies and tax shelters.

Corporate income taxes are levied by the federal and state governments on business profits (Sales minus Costs of doing business). There are two different types of corporations (C-Corp and S-Corp) and they are taxed differently. It will be discussed under the Business Structure section of this chapter.

Payroll taxes are taxes paid on the wages and salaries of employees to finance social insurance programs. You will see this tax on your paystub. Half of this tax is paid by your employer while the other half is paid by you through payroll withholdings. Currently, the tax is 15.3% (12.4% funds Social Security, 2.9% funds Medicare) so you as an individual taxpayer pay 7.65%.

Capital Gains tax as explained above is paid on income from the sale or exchange of assets such as stock or property that is categorized as a capital asset.

Second type: Tax on what you purchase

Sales Taxes are a form of consumption tax levied on retail sales of goods and services. You are familiar with this tax because this is printed at the bottom of store receipts. This tax is a significant source of revenue for state and local jurisdictions. If you want to learn more about this topic, you can go to the IRS website and locate Publication 600.

Gross Receipts Taxes are applied to a company's gross sales, regardless of their profitability and without deductions for business expenses, unlike other taxes that businesses pay such as corporate income tax.

Value-Added Taxes are a consumption tax assessed on the value that is added in each production stage of goods or services. Each business along the production chain pays VAT on the value of the good/service at that stage, with the VAT previously paid for that good/service being deductible at each step. The final consumer pays the VAT without being able to deduct the previously paid VAT which makes this a tax on final consumption. More than 140 countries except the U.S. levy a VAT.

Excise Taxes are taxes imposed on specific goods or activities. Common examples are those on cigarettes, alcohol, soda/sugary drinks, gasoline, airfare, telecommunication services, indoor tanning, and gambling. Excise tax can be employed as user fees. An example would be the gas tax because the amount of gas a driver purchase reflects their contribution to traffic congestion and road wear-and-tear. Excise tax can also be employed as a "sin" tax to offset externalities. Governments may place a special tax on cigarettes with the hope of reducing consumption.

Third type: Tax on what you own

Property Taxes are levied on immovable property like land and buildings and it's an essential source of revenue for state and local governments. Local governments rely on property tax revenue to fund public services like roads, schools, police and fire departments, and emergency medical services.

Tangible Personal Property (TPP) Taxes are levied on property that can be moved or touched such as business equipment, machinery, furniture, automobiles, and inventory. This tax makes up a small share of the total state and local tax collections.

Estate and Inheritance Taxes are imposed on the value of an individual's property at the time of his or her death. Estate taxes are paid by the estate itself before the assets are distributed to the heirs. The federal estate tax exemption for the year 2020 is $11.58 million. Some states use the same exemption amount as the federal. The state of Massachusetts has one of the lowest exemptions, at only $1 million. Inheritance taxes are paid by those who inherit the property. There is no federal inheritance tax. Only six states collect this. The state of Maryland collects both an estate and inheritance tax. The tax rate depends on how much you inherit and your relationship to the deceased.

Wealth Taxes are imposed annually on an individual's net wealth (total assets minus liabilities) above a certain threshold. As of 2019, only six countries in Europe had a wealth tax because they are difficult to administer, has harmful effects on the economy, and discourage entrepreneurship and innovation.

Tariffs are not part of the third type of tax but worth mentioning here. Tariffs are taxes on goods that cross national borders. The country importing the goods collects the tariffs. This is a way for the government to bolster local businesses and to level the playing field with foreign competition.

Tax Deductions vs. Tax Credit

When you file your tax return do you know which items are "tax-deductible" items and which are "tax credit" items? Your tax deduction items are the expenses you deduct to come up with your taxable income which is the amount you will pay tax on. These deductions are reported in your tax return Form 1040, Schedule A if you are itemizing your deduction (see appendix). Tax credits on the other hand reduce the tax you owe dollar-for-dollar. Unfortunately, most tax credits are not well understood by millions of Americans.

Some of the common tax credits are, child tax credit, credit for other dependents, child and dependent care credit, earned income tax credit, lifetime learning credit, saver's tax credit, federal adoption tax credit, residential energy-efficient property credit, foreign tax credit, and plug-in electric-drive motor vehicle credit.

Tax treatment on various investment accounts

How much tax are you paying on earnings from your investments, do you know? The following topic is important as I will be explaining how different investment accounts are taxed. If your money is in checking, savings, CDs, stock, or mutual funds, you earn interest income and dividend income which is taxed in the year you received them. Every year, your financial institution mails you Form 1099-INT and/or 1099-DIV. The form shows the amount of interest and/or dividend you received in the year so you can report this income in your tax return. These are called **"Tax Now"** vehicles.

If you are putting away a portion of your salary to a retirement plan at work such as 401(k) or 403(b), the money you are putting in the account is pre-tax. It hasn't been taxed yet, which means when you make a withdrawal from these types of accounts, you will have to pay tax, and possibly a penalty of 10% if you are not 59 ½ or older at the time of the withdrawal. However, due to COVID-19, certain rules affect this, so make sure you understand the current tax treatment. Other investment vehicles such as IRA, SEP-IRA, SIMPLE IRA, Annuities, and Pension are examples of **"Tax-Deferred"** vehicles.

Other types of investments are the **"Tax Advantaged"** vehicles where the money you put into the accounts is post-tax dollars – it has already been taxed. Examples of this type: Roth IRA, 529 College Plans, Coverdell Plans, Municipal Bonds, and Cash Value Life Insurance. Note that only individuals with income below a threshold level can contribute to ROTH IRA thus people turn to Cash Value Life Insurance to create sources of tax-free future income.

Which of these categories (Tax Now, Tax-Deferred, Tax Advantaged), have you been putting your money in? Based on what you just read, should you be diversifying your investment so that not all of it is in one category thus mitigating your tax risk?

Tax on the SEED vs. Tax on the HARVEST?

You just learned the difference between "Tax-Deferred" versus "Tax-Advantaged" investments. When you contribute to a Tax-Deferred vehicle such as IRA or 401(k), your contribution is pre-tax. You have not paid tax on it. You allow those pre-tax dollars to grow over several years and then when it's time to retire you take the distribution and get taxed at that time. Nobody knows what the tax will be when you take the distribution. This scenario is an example of "Tax on the Harvest"

When you contribute to a Tax-Advantaged vehicle such as ROTH IRA your contribution is post-tax. You already paid tax on it. You allow those post-tax dollars to grow over several years, and then when it's time to retire you take distributions and you never have to worry about paying tax at that time. This scenario is an example of "Tax on the Seed"

Later on, I will show you how you can convert your IRA or 401(k) to a ROTH IRA so you never have to worry about what the tax rate will be when you take distribution upon retirement. What if history repeats itself at the time you retire, and the marginal tax rate is 94%? I think you have an important decision to make.

As always, my suggestion is to consult with someone who can help you crunch the number and take action.

Income Tax vs. Capital Gain Tax

Do you know the difference between Income tax and capital gain tax? Income tax is paid on earnings from wages, salaries, commissions, interest, dividends, royalties, or self-employment. Capital gain tax on the other hand is paid on income from the sale or exchange of assets such as stock or property that is categorized as a capital asset. The income tax rates range from 10% to 37% and it rises as income rises.

Short term capital gains are treated as ordinary income when assets are held for one year or less. Long-term capital gains have preferential rates of 0%, 15%, or 20% depending on the income level.

In the previous chapter, I spoke about cash flow quadrants and how people on the right side (Business Owner's and Investors) are paying less tax than the people on the left side (Employees and Self-Employed) even though the people on the right make substantially more than the ones on the left and that's because Business Owners and Investors have businesses where they take advantage of tax deductions and tax credits, which are the two ways to get into a lower tax bracket. Tax credits are a dollar for dollar reduction in your income tax bill and they can save you more in taxes than tax deductions because tax deductions only reduce the amount of your income that is taxable. Later, I will discuss tax credits that you as an individual taxpayer can take.

Business Structures

There are different types of business structures. Some of the factors which can influence your decision to choose a type over another are, taxes the company will be subject to pay, who will be qualified to own the company, day to day operations, your liability, compliance requirements, desire to minimize self-employment tax obligation, registration, and administration fees. The popular types of business structures are Sole Proprietorship, Partnership, Limited Liability Company (LLC), S-Corporation, and C-Corporation.

Sole proprietorships do not produce a separate business entity. The business assets and liabilities are not separate from their owners' personal assets and liabilities. You can be held personally liable for the debts of the business.

It will be hard to raise money with this structure because there's no stock, and banks are hesitant to lend.

A **partnership** is when two or more people own a business together. It can be a limited partnership (LP) or limited liability partnerships (LLP). LPs have must have one general with unlimited liability while the others have limited liability whereas, in LLP, all owners have limited liability. Profits are passed through to personal tax returns and the general partner must also pay self-employment taxes. If you want to learn more about Partnership, you can go to the IRS website and locate Publication 541.

Limited Liability Company (LLC) takes advantage of the benefits of both the corporation and partnership business structures. LLC's protect owners from personal liability and in most instances, personal assets won't be at risk in case LLC faces lawsuits. Profits and losses can get passed through to personal income without facing corporates taxes, but members of an LLC are considered self-employed so they must pay self-employment tax. If you want to learn more about LLCs, you can go to the IRS website and locate Publication 3402.

The **C-Corporation** is a legal entity that is separate from its owners. This entity type offers the strongest protection for its owners from a personal liability standpoint. However, the cost to form a C-corp is higher than other structures and they also require more extensive record-keeping, operational processes, and reporting. Corporate profits are taxed twice, first at the company level, and then when shareholders receive dividends. Raising capital is easier with this structure because they can sell stocks. The federal corporate tax rate currently is a flat 21%.

The **S-Corporation** is an entity type designed to avoid double taxation. Profits and losses are passed through to the owner's income without ever being subject to corporate tax. Not all states tax S-corps like the federal government. Some states tax S corps on profits above a specified limit while other states don't recognize the S-corp election at all. Those states treat it like a C-corp. S-corps cannot have more than 100 shareholders, and all shareholders must be U.S. citizens. Like C-corps, they have strict filing requirements and operational processes.

If you want to learn more about Corporation, you can go to the IRS website and locate Publication 542.

Congratulations! Now that you have a good understanding of the Rate of Return, how important time is in investing, how different investment vehicles are taxed, and the difference between paying tax on the seed vs. the harvest, you can assess whether your current plan is the most tax-efficient.

CHAPTER 4
THE STRATEGIES

The strategies presented here may or may not apply to you, but I want you to understand that they exist as you may be able to utilize them now or in the future. I want to remind you again to take a pen and pad and be sure to make notes of some of the strategies presented here that may work for you. As always, consult with an expert who can help you decide the right strategy for your unique situation. Some of the strategies presented here are from various continuing professional education webinars I've attended as well as the strategies I learned from NY Life Securities / New York Life.

Backdoor Roth IRA

ROTH IRA as you already know is a Tax-Advantaged vehicle that allows you to contribute with your post-tax dollars and will not have to pay tax on the qualified distribution. Every year you can only contribute a certain amount. In the current tax law, you can contribute up to $6K ($7K if you are 50 or older) however this amount is phased out when your income reaches a certain amount.

There are ways around this contribution limit. If you contribute to a non-deductible IRA or nondeductible contributions to a 401(k) plan, you can convert it to a ROTH IRA.

Charitable Remainder Trust (CRT)

This Charitable Remainder Trust strategy is used to secure a lifetime income, save on taxes, and provide benefits to a charity. This CRT strategy allows you to convert a highly appreciated asset such as stocks or real estate into a lifetime income. This helps reduce your income taxes now and your estate taxes when you die. You pay no capital gains tax when the asset is sold because trust is exempt from capital gains tax and you help one or more of your favorite charities. How this works is that you will transfer an appreciated asset into an irrevocable trust which removes the asset from your estate, so that there are no estate taxes due when you die. You will receive an immediate charitable income tax deduction.

When the trustee sells the asset at full market value, it will pay no capital gains tax, and it will re-invest the proceeds in income-producing assets. For the rest of your life, the trust pays you an income. When you die the remaining trust assets go to the charity you have chosen.

Domestic Asset Protection Trust (DAPT)

Domestic Asset Protection Trust is a type of irrevocable trust that allows you to be the beneficiary. It operates very similar to a spendthrift trust, which allows you to establish a trust for yourself so you can have full control over how the money is spent. It can be set up in certain states to protect your assets in the event of future creditors' actions and lawsuits. You can use it to transfer a variety of assets, such as cash, real estate, securities, and business interests. Not everyone needs this. Those who work in high-risk professions, such as physicians, lawyers, CEOs, and others with a high net worth may benefit from the asset protection that this offers. Also, even though this offers protection from creditors, this should be set up before facing a creditor judgment, because once it's set up, the assets are not immediately protected. Each state has a statute of limitations which can be several years or longer.

Dynasty Trust

Dynasty trust is similar to the ILIT strategy, so basically, you transfer assets such as a farm or cash, into a trust and purchase a life insurance policy. The beneficiaries of that trust will not have a right to the principal. Instead, they will receive income distributions. With proper care and management, those assets will continue to provide income to future generations. Additionally, the principal will receive creditor protection, ex-spouse protection, and remain outside the taxable estates for future generations and beneficiaries.

Grantor Retained Annuity Trust (GRAT)

A grantor retained annuity trust is a type of irrevocable gifting trust that allows a grantor to potentially pass a significant amount of wealth to the next generation with little or no gift tax cost. GRATs are established for a specific number of years and are most useful to wealthy individuals who face significant estate tax liability at death. GRAT may be used to freeze the value of their estate by shifting a portion or all the appreciation on to their heirs.

Incomplete Non-Grantor Trust (ING)

The Incomplete Non-Grantor Trust is an asset protection trust that provides income tax benefits to grantors residing in a state with high state income tax rates or a state that does not recognize the federal grantor trust rules. This trust allows a grantor to fund the trust without incurring gift tax while also achieving non-grantor status for income tax purposes. There are several tax benefits but the most notable is the state income tax savings for grantors living in high-income tax states. The grantor ideally transfers appreciated assets with a low basis into the trust. Because the ING trust is established in a low or no-income-tax state, the sale of these assets is subject to minimal state income tax. The grantor can transfer assets into a trust, retain access to the cash flow, and avoid making a completed gift for federal give tax consequences. This is appealing to individuals that have already fully utilize their lifetime gift tax exemption.

Intentionally Defective Grantor Trust (IDGT)

This strategy is an estate-planning tool that is used to freeze certain assets of an individual for estate-tax purposes, but not for income tax purposes. It is effectively a grantor trust with a purposeful flaw that ensures the individual continues to pay income taxes. The beneficiaries of IDGTs are typically children or grandchildren who will receive assets that have been able to grow without reductions for income taxes, which the grantor has paid. The IDGT can be a very effective estate-planning tool if structured properly, allowing a person to lower his or her taxable estate while gifting assets to beneficiaries at a locked-in value. The trust's grantor can also lower his or her taxable estate by paying income taxes on the trust assets, essentially gifting extra wealth to beneficiaries.

Irrevocable Life Insurance Trust (ILIT)

This strategy is used in estate and asset protection planning. Life insurance is normally taxable for federal estate tax purposes so if you die owning $1 Million of life insurance at the time of your death, the value of the life insurance is included in your taxable estate. If you have a spouse and he/she is the beneficiary, then the proceeds are exempt from estate tax because of the unlimited marital deduction. However, on your spouse's death, any remaining proceeds will be included in their estate, possibly subject to probate, and only have the applicable exclusion amount as an exemption. An Irrevocable Life Insurance Trust is a strategy used in estate and asset protection planning. This trust cannot be changed or canceled. When life insurance policies are transferred to this trust, the proceeds received under the policy can be kept out of your and your spouse's estate if the trust is drafted correctly. The irrevocable nature of the trust offers insulation of the trust policies from the claims of your creditors. The policy must be transferred to the trust for more than three years before death. You may not have any incidents of ownership in the policy nor the right to direct economic enjoyment of the trust. Also, you should not be named as a trustee since, as a trustee, you may have retained an incident of ownership or the power to direct an economic benefit of the policy.

Medicaid Trust

An Irrevocable Medicaid trust is a planning strategy whereas older people can put their assets into the trust so the government cannot count those assets for Medicaid qualification purposes. They can still live in the house, use the furniture, and drive the car held by the trust. Generally, there's a provision in the trust so that the children and/or grandkids can receive the assets after passing. This is also a strategy to help older people protect their assets from nursing homes. Transfers to Medicaid trusts must generally be made at least 36 months before the person enters a nursing home.

Multi-Generational Legacy

This is an intra-family loan strategy that preserves gift and estate tax exclusions while creating an asset to be used for education, retirement, or estate purposes. The grandparents' loan money to their child to purchase life insurance on the child's life. The loan is made in exchange for an interest-bearing promissory note governed by the split-dollar loan regime. The loan repayments can be used to fund grandparents' retirement or long-term care needs. After loan repayment, the child can access policy cash values to fund retirement or other life events. The income tax-free death benefit will be available for the benefit of the grandchildren.

Partial Roth Conversions

In chapter 3 I discussed Tax on the Seed versus Tax on the Harvest whereas Tax on the Seed is when you pay tax on the distribution from your Tax-Deferred accounts (i.e. IRA/401(k)) while Tax on the Harvest is when you don't pay tax on the distribution from your Tax-Advantaged accounts (ROTH). Currently, we have about $31Trillion in the Qualified plan (i.e. 401(k), 403(b), IRA) waiting to be taxed by Uncle Sam.

In the current tax law, anyone with pre-tax retirement accounts (IRA/401(k)) can convert to a ROTH IRA or ROTH 401(k) and pay tax on the distribution. It is up to the investor/taxpayer to decide whether to convert everything or partial accounts. This is not going to be a simple analysis and calculation so make sure you seek the guidance of your CPA and calculate what would be the right amount to convert because once you convert, it is permanent. This strategy again is to accelerate income, pay tax now to avoid paying higher taxes in the future. You may have to do this analysis every year if you did not convert 100% to figure out what amount would make sense to be transferred to ROTH accounts.

If you are one of those people who think that you will have a lower tax rate when you take the distribution, think again. The Required Minimum Distribution (RMD) may push you to the higher tax brackets.

Again, the goal of partial ROTH conversion is to find a balance whereas the converted amount is low enough to avoid top tax rates today, but not so little that the remaining retirement account balance plus the compounding growth will cause it to be exposed to top tax brackets in the future. You need to find the right balance.

Premarital Agreements

Premarital agreements are becoming popular as more and more people realize the economic and emotional problems that result from a divorce. This is a contract between parties who intend to marry. The agreement can cover various topics but the issue that is commonly dealt with is the separate property and income of each party, the division of property upon divorce, and support obligations upon divorce.

Set for Life Strategy

Set for Life strategy is a strategy where, the parents or grandparents of a baby purchase a life insurance policy for the child to provide lifetime protection, to establish affordability, access cash values, and create a legacy for the child. When this policy is funded properly, the child can take tax-free withdrawals for college tuition, a down payment to start a business, or supplemental retirement income.

The child would still have a death benefit left for his or her heirs. All the withdrawals are tax-free.

Spendthrift Trust

A spendthrift trust is an irrevocable living trust that's overseen by a trustee on an ongoing basis from the time of its inception and continuing after the death of the grantor. It continues to hold its assets for incremental distribution to the beneficiaries. The idea behind this is so that it prevents certain beneficiaries from receiving their inheritances all at once. It is distributed over time to keep beneficiaries from potentially wasting the entire inheritance at once. This is also a strategy to protect the money from the beneficiary's creditors. The beneficiary has no right to the money and cannot spend it before receiving the distributions. Creditors can only reach the money that the beneficiary has actually received, and not the portion of the inheritance that remains in the trust.

Spousal Limited Access Trust (SLAT)

The Spousal Limited Asset Trust can be an effective estate planning tool for a wealthy married couple who wishes to reduce estate taxes, protect their assets from creditors, or both. This is an irrevocable trust created by one spouse for the benefit of the other spouse. The donor spouse uses their gift tax exemption to make a gift to the SLAT for the benefit of his or her spouse. The donor spouse gives up his or her right to the property transferred into the trust while the beneficiary spouse maintains access to that same property. The fundamental goal is to get assets into a trust that can provide financial support to a beneficiary while sheltering those assets and any future growth from an estate and gift tax.

Business Gift & Estate Equalization

This strategy will work in circumstances where a business owner's future desire is to transfer the business by gift or bequest to a child who desires to get involved and eventually take over the business. To be fair to the other children who will not inherit the business, the business owner can own an insurance policy and name those children his/her beneficiaries on the permanent life insurance policy.

Business Owner Retirement Solution

The Supplemental Life Insurance Retirement Plan is a strategy whereas the business owner purchases a life insurance policy and pays a premium before retirement. Once retired, he/she can withdraw monthly income or borrow against the policy. Upon death, the beneficiaries receive the benefit income tax-free.

Buy-Sell Agreements

Any business owner should have an exit strategy. Owners should evaluate what happens to the business upon death and have a plan for its sale or continued operation. If two or more people own a small business, a buy-sell agreement strategy is an absolute necessity. This is an agreement for the disposition of the business interest in the event of the owner's death, disability, divorce, or retirement.

Captive Insurance Strategy

This is a strategy used by ultra-high net worth individuals to supplement their current insurance program in a tax-efficient manner. This is a form of self-insurance. Instead of paying money to an insurance provider in exchange for financial protection, you pay the premium to your own insurance company, allow the premiums to accumulate in the account, and pay for any claims from that account. You will need to establish your own insurance company to cover the risks associated with your business. Some of the benefits are, you get to keep your premium payments, reduce your tax burden, protect your business, and make a tax-efficient withdrawal.

Conservation Easements

Before I can explain Conservation Easement Strategy, let me first explain what a Conservation Land Trust is. There are two types of land trust: a title-holding trust and a conservation land trust. The former allows the property owner to anonymously maintains all rights over the property and direct the actions of the land trust, kind of like what Walt Disney did when he acquired the Florida swamplands (where Walt Disney World is built) from the original owners. The latter trust on the other hand requires that the property owner give up some rights over land use and development. The goal of conservation trust is to protect wildlife, historical or cultural sites, and natural resources from commercial development or other activities that may lead to disruption or pollution.

In a conservation land trust, the trust doesn't take over the land title unless the property is donated in its entirety. Instead, a landowner enters into a legally binding agreement, called conservation easement, donating their development rights to the trust. If a landowner donates their development rights to a conservation trust, they can receive a tax deduction equal to the difference between the land value as encumbered, and what it could be worth if it were developed for its "highest and best use". The deduction can be worth millions of dollars.

However, an investment niche has developed designed to open the tax benefits of conservation to a larger portion of the population.

By using a multi-member partnership, these investment companies allowed multiple accredited investors to pool their money to purchase land for conservation. After donating the property development rights to a land trust via conservation easement, the members of the partnership split the tax deduction pro-rata. Of course, whenever there is potential for profit, someone will abuse the system. Currently, there have been some high-profile cases of people taking exceptionally large deductions for donating easements on golf courses, housing developments, and other properties that don't actually have much ecological or cultural value.

Cost Segregation Study

This Cost Segregation Study is a strategy used by commercial and residential rental property owners to significantly reduce taxable income and increase cash flow. The process of cost segregation begins at the time of purchase. An engineering study is done to segregate assets into four categories: personal property, land improvements, buildings, and land. This allows the purchaser to achieve faster depreciation deductions as well as possible and easier subsequent write-offs, so its cash flow will be increased. Assets allocated into the first two categories are depreciated shorter lives, thus, accelerated depreciation methods. Also, if the components of a building have been separately valued and a component subsequently becomes worthless, they can write it off more easily.

Employee Stock Ownership Plan (ESOP)

ESOP is a kind of employee benefit plan similar to a profit-sharing plan. A company sets up a trust fund to which it contributes new shares of its own stock or cash to buy existing shares. This is used to create an additional employee benefit, to borrow money at a lower after-tax cost, and to buy the shares of a departing owner. Some of the tax benefits are, the contributions of stock are tax-deductible, cash contributions are deductible, the contributions used to repay a loan the ESOP takes to buy company shares are tax-deductible, the sellers in a C-corporation can get a tax deferral, dividends are tax-deductible, and employees pay no tax on the contributions to the ESOP plan.

Family Limited Partnership (FLP)

This Family Limited Partnership strategy is commonly set up to preserve generational wealth within a family, allowing for tax-free transfers of assets, real estate, and other wealth. This is a type of arrangement whereas family members pool money to run a business project. Each family member buys units or shares of the business and can profit in proportion to the number of shares he/she owns as outlined in the partnership operating agreement. Every year, an individual can gift FLP interests tax-free to other individuals up to the annual gift tax exclusion.

Installment Sales

An installment sale strategy can permit a taxpayer to pay his taxes on the disposition of property as he receives the payments. This deferral can result in huge tax savings. The basic requirements are, there must be a sale of a property, the property must not be of a kind which is required to be included in the inventory of the taxpayer if on hand at the close of the taxable year, and there must be an installment sale. If you want to learn more about this topic, you can go to the IRS website and locate Publication 537.

Opportunity Zone

The Tax Cuts and Jobs Act included this federal incentive to spur investment in undercapitalized communities. Any corporation or individual with capital gains can quality.

This program provides three tax benefits: (1) investors can place an existing asset with accumulated capital gains into Opportunity Funds. Those existing capital gains are not taxed until the end of 2026 or when the asset is disposed of, (2) for capital gains placed in Opportunity Funds for at least 5 years, the investor's basis on the original investment increases by 10%. That percentage increases to 15% if invested for at least 7 years, and (3)for investments held for at least 10 years, investors pay no taxes on any capital gains produced through their investment in Opportunity Funds.

Qualified Small Business Stock - Sec. 1202

How do you like owning stock in a company where the price appreciates, and then when you sell it, you pay no tax on your profit? Too good to be true? Check IRC Section 1202. This is a planning tool for the right company such as a tech start-up. If you have a C corporation or are thinking of forming one, and you are in an eligible industry, then consider using QSBS to raise capital or compensate key employees. The conditions that must be met are the following, the issuer must be a C corporation whose assets do not exceed over $50 million on or after the issuance of stock, and only certain types of companies fall under the category of a qualified small business. Companies in technology, retail, wholesale, and manufacturing are eligible.

Research and Development (R&D) Tax Credits

The purpose of this R&D tax credit is to reward U.S. companies for increasing their investment in R&D in the current tax year. It is available to any business that attempts to develop new, improved, or technologically advanced products or trade processes. The research tax credit was first established in 1981 to reward companies for their investment in research and development activities and expenditures. It is an incremental credit based on a company's increase in spending on R&D, with qualified expenditures known as Qualified Research Expenses (QRE). For most companies claiming an R&D tax credit, the largest QREs relate to wages paid to employees for time spent conducting qualifying R&D activities.

Sec. 1031 Like-Kind Exchange

The Like-Kind Exchange strategy allows the real estate owner to move from one property to another without reducing equity build-up by income taxes due on any gain. The basic requirements are: the properties must be exchanged and not sold, both the property exchanged and the property received must be held for productive use in trade, business, or for investment, and the properties must be of a "like-kind" with one another.

SERP Plan

Supplemental Executive Retirement Plan (SERP) is a strategy used by companies to reward, retain, and incentivize their key executives. This is a non-qualified plan which means it doesn't need IRS approval, unlike a 401(k)plan. Typically, the company and the executive sign an agreement that promises the executive a certain amount of supplemental retirement income based on various eligibility conditions that the executive must meet. The company then funds the plan out of its cash flows or through the funding of a cash value life insurance policy. Note though that the funds accumulated inside the policy are not protected from the creditor's claim against the company in case of its insolvency. The other disadvantage is that the company can only deduct business expenses when the benefits are paid to the executive.

Split-Dollar Arrangement

This is a method of purchasing life insurance in which premium payments, policy benefits, or both are divided in some predetermined way between the business owner and an employee. This can be an effective method of attracting and retaining valuable key employees. The employer may have access to the policy's cash value, and this can provide much-needed insurance protection for the employee, therefore, creating dual benefit.

Congratulations! You just learned unbelievably valuable information you can use to properly structure your finances which will help you protect your assets from creditors and pay less or no taxes legally.

CHAPTER 5
THE GAP

Just to recap what we've done so far, in Chapter 1, we've gone over some of the limiting beliefs and negative programming you may have about money, the importance of using emotional intelligence in achieving your goals, and why you should follow your heart, not your brain. In Chapter 2, we've gone over some of the fundamentals surrounding money and you established a clear goal. In Chapter 3, we have gone over some of the tax and financial concepts. In Chapter 4, we've gone over some of the strategies that ultra-high-net-worth-individuals and businesses utilize to minimize taxes. In this Chapter, we will closely look at where you are financially, where you want to be, and show you how to close the gap. I will also share some of the goals I've set for myself, my family, and my businesses.

Net Profit & Net Worth

Earlier you learned what an Income Statement is and what gets reported there. You also learned the formula to get to your Net Profit or Net Income/Loss amount. The Net Profit / Net Income formula again is the sum of your Income and Gains from the sale of assets, minus the sum of your Expenses and Losses from the sale of assets.

You also learned what a Balance Sheet is and what gets reported there. You learned the formula Assets = Liabilities + Equity or Assets − Liabilities = Equity or Net Worth (add up all of your assets and subtract all of your liabilities to come up with your Net Worth amount).

Now that you have your Net Profit and Net Worth amounts, the next step is to review the goals you've set. Depending on where you're in your financial life stage, your goal could be to protect yourself, your family, and your assets from unexpected death or illness. Your goal could be to purchase your first car or home, to plan for early retirement, to buy real estate investments, to buy a business, or to accumulate more assets. Whatever it may be, I hope that the examples below will guide you in the right direction.

Everyone's situation is different, but now that you understand the fundamentals, the various concepts, and strategies available, you should be proud of yourself because you are better off than most of the people who don't understand what you just learned. Later, you will learn concepts about Life Insurance, Annuities, General Securities, and Real Estate, but for now, let's look at some of the example goals that people set for themselves.

Sample Goal: Plan to purchase your first car or first house

By knowing your monthly net income amount from your Income Statement, you'll be able to decide if you're able to take on another expense. If you can't do so, then you can focus on saving more so you can put down a larger deposit which will reduce the amount you have to borrow. You can also focus on increasing your monthly income. Hopefully, you have good credit and have the leverage to negotiate a competitive interest rate.

Sample Goal: Income Replacement Planning

Why is it that we carry all kinds of insurance (health, auto, home, phone, home warranty), but some of you are not protecting yourself by having enough life insurance coverage? Unless you're working with a financial planner, received a call from a life insurance agent, or you purchased a home and you received a letter in the mail asking you to apply for term insurance to protect your newly purchased home, you probably didn't think to call an insurance agent just to purchase a life insurance policy, right? Many people wait to call an insurance agent until it's too late and harder for you to get good life insurance coverage. Your options become limited as you get older, and you may be just one doctor visit away from not being approved for one.

Your income is one of your greatest financial assets, so if you were gone tomorrow, would your family and loved ones have enough financial security to live comfortably for the next 10 years? I had the opportunity to work for some of the big insurance companies and I learned a lot. I wish I knew some of the things I learned sooner. Later, I will explain different types of life insurance. For now, you should start thinking about how much coverage you and your family require. There's a Need Analysis form that life insurance agents complete to help clients figure out the total amount of protection they need. Make sure you understand how the different types of insurance work before you apply.

I have a funny story to tell you about my life insurance policies. No one came knocking at my door or called me to offer life insurance, but I wish somebody had because I would've learned this strategy sooner and bought a lot more than what I currently have. When I purchased my second house after I sold the first, I received a letter from a life insurance company offering a life policy for the same amount as the price I paid for the home. My third purchase was a rental property, and again I received a letter from a life insurance company offering a life policy for the same amount as the price I paid for it as an intended rental. This happened two more times, so I accumulated four different policies. I was young when I got these policies, so the premium was very inexpensive. I just kept them all and I'm glad I did.

I encourage Millennials and Gen Z to purchase a permanent life insurance policy while you're young, and if you can afford a whole life policy contract from a mutual life insurance company, even better. The owners of a Mutual life insurance company are the policyholders, which means you receive dividends. There are so many strategies you can use with a whole life policy that you cannot with other types. Other than additional growth through dividends, the other benefits are, guaranteed cash value growth, the premium is guaranteed never to increase, guaranteed death benefit, income tax-free death benefit, tax-free access to cash values, protection from creditors in some states, and tax-deferred cash value growth. There is no vehicle out there that can accomplish all these.

I encourage grandparents and parents who have newborns to purchase a whole life policy as this will make the baby set for the rest of his/her life. It will provide lifetime protection. The premiums will never increase. The child generally will have tax-free access to the cash values for life events such as a first car, college tuition, start-up funds for a business, and help with retirement. This will also give the child the ability to leave a legacy for his/her future heirs and set them up with a tax-free death benefit for their needs.

Whole life policies are not for everyone since they are expensive. Other types are Universal Life and Term Life Insurance policies. If you don't own life insurance yet, you should take care of this as soon as possible because you'll just never know what can happen to you. You want to make sure that the income you're bringing into your household will be replaced in case something happens because the bills will not stop coming when you're gone or become disabled.

Life insurance is not something that anybody can get. It's not your money that buys life insurance, it's your health. If your health is not so good, you will have a hard time finding a reputable insurance company to offer you excellent coverage. Even if they offer you coverage, your premium will be substantially high. Mom passed away when she was only 54 of breast cancer. When she was diagnosed, this is one of the things she taught us, to invest in life insurance. Fortunately, when she told us this, I already own multiple policies.

Now, look at your monthly Income Statement to see how much life insurance premium you can afford to pay every month, and then do reverse engineering to find out how much life insurance coverage you will get for an X amount of premium paid each month. If the life insurance coverage is not enough to protect your family in case of death/disability, then find a way to generate additional income by starting a part-time business.

Sample Goal: Plan for Children's Education

Depending on your child's age, if they're young enough, then you should consider the "Set for Life" strategy as I explained above. The second option would be the 529 college savings plan. This is a tax-advantaged plan which means you don't get taxed when you take the money out of the plan as long as it's for education-related expenses. The biggest drawback though is that colleges consider this when deciding on financial aid, which means your child could receive less financial aid, but the effect should be minimal and shouldn't deter you from using this as a way to save. Up to 5.64% of the value of the plan owned by the parent or dependent student will be included in the student's Expected Family Contribution. This plan is a lot like ROTH IRA. It's designed for education expenses rather than retirement. This plan was originally used to cover post-secondary education costs, but this was changed to include K-12 under the Tax Cuts and Jobs Act.

The third option would be a Coverdell ESA. They get the same tax-advantage as 529's on the federal level however, your state isn't going to let you write-off Coverdell contributions. They are not state-run, so if you live in a state that offers deductions for 529 contributions, then this can be a big difference. You can contribute to both plans at the same time as long as the combined annual contribution does not exceed the annual gift tax exclusion amount which is $15,000 currently. Another difference is that, when you use a 529 plan for elementary and secondary schools, it is limited to tuition only while the Coverdell can pay for tuition and other school expenses. As always, my suggestion is to consult with someone who can help you decide the right strategy for your situation.

The other strategy that may work is if the child has a divorced parent. The child applies for the student loan using the parent's tax return who has lesser income so that the child can qualify for student loans or grants. Instead of paying for their tuition, put that money away into a vehicle that is safe, has growth potential, and overpowers inflation because when your child graduates, you'll take that money and pay off 100% of their student loan. Doing this allows you to make use of the government money while the child is in school and then give it back when the child graduates. Your situation has to be right for this strategy to work. The child must qualify for student loans, or else they won't be able to get a loan and you have to be very disciplined to put that money away.

Sample Goal: Plan for Early Retirement

There are various ways to save for retirement. As explained in the previous chapter, if your employer is offering a matching program on your 401k plan, make sure you take advantage of that free money given to you by contributing up to their matching percentage. For example, if the company is matching up to 5%, then you need to contribute at least 5% to the plan. The rule of thumb is to contribute at least 10% of your pay and sign up for auto-escalation so you contribute slightly more each year. Other tax-deferred plans are IRA, SEP IRA, and SIMPLE. They are tax-deferred plans because the funds you contributed have not been taxed yet so when you take a distribution from these plans later, you will get taxed not only on the funds you contributed but also from their growth. If you are less than 59 ½ at the time of distribution, there will be a 10% penalty.

You can also put money in tax-advantaged vehicles such as ROTH IRA and Cash Value Life Insurance. ROTH IRA contributions are not tax-deductible, but your earnings can grow tax-free and any "qualified" withdrawals are tax and penalty-free. You can also use a whole life insurance strategy by funding it with the intent of taking annual withdrawals as a loan during your retirement. If you don't pay the loan back, the insurance company will just deduct the loan before they pay out the death benefit to your beneficiaries.

Which one do you think is better in your scenario, tax-deferred, or tax-advantaged plans? Perhaps you can diversify risk and allocate some funds in tax-deferred and some in tax-advantaged plans. If you're an employee you can contribute up to the employer's matching percentage, the rest of the available money can go to ROTH IRA and/or purchase additional cash value life insurance, and let the money grow tax-free.

Then decide on starting a part-time business that you will enjoy doing and grow that business to the point you can leave your job. In the earlier chapter, I explained the cash flow quadrant. I hope your goal is to get to the right quadrant because the B's and I's are the people who pay less or no tax at all. They have structures in place so that their plan is tax efficient. Everyone's situation is different. You are planning for your future so I suggest you consult with a professional who can look at your whole financial picture and help you make a decision.

Since we're on the topic of retirement, I think it's important that you understand and remember important milestones under the current tax law:

Age 50, there's a catch-up provision that allows for greater contribution to a qualified plan.

Age 55, if retired, you can begin 401(k) withdrawals without penalty

Age 59 ½, one can withdraw tax-deferred assets without penalty

Age 62, is the first year of social security eligibility

Age 65, is the first year of Medicare benefit eligibility

Age 66/67, is the full social security benefit under the current law

Age 70, is the age of maximum social security benefit eligibility

Age 70 ½, is when one is required to begin taking required minimum distributions (RMD's)

Sample Goal: Asset Acquisition

This is an excellent goal to have. To build wealth, you either must create or purchase assets and keep doing that over and over. There are two types of categories of assets, tangible and intangible. The Accounting Principles book by Larson/Pyle defines intangible assets as assets having no physical existence but rather, they represent certain legal rights and economic relationships that are beneficial to the owner. Examples are goodwill, patents, copyrights, and trademarks. Tangible assets are physical assets that companies use to produce their product or service. Examples are inventory, equipment, and buildings.

How do you create an asset or intellectual property? You can write a song, write a book, develop an e-course, invent the machine, create a proprietary process, etc. If you're an inventor, you can patent your invention. A patent will give you the exclusive right to use, manufacture, and sell a product or process for a period of time without interference or infringement by others. If you write a book or song, you can copyright it. A copyright is a federally granted right that all authors, painters, musicians, sculptors, and other artists have in their creations and expressions. You can start a business and have a proprietary process and allow others to use that proprietary knowledge through franchise licensing. A franchise is a contractual arrangement under which the franchisor grants the franchisee the right to sell certain products or services, to use certain trademarks and trade names, or to perform certain functions, within a designated geographical area. You can purchase assets such as equipment, machinery, vehicles, residential or commercial real properties and lease them.

Sample Goal: Business Acquisition

To purchase an established and profitable business is a great goal to have. Doing this will put you on the right side of Robert Kiyosaki's cash flow quadrant where the Business Owners and Investors are. One of the many hats I wear is a Business Broker/Intermediary. I help facilitate the sale of a private business with annual revenue of up to $10M. When I work with the sellers, I help them get organized to maximize the value of their business. I help them set a price based on the data from comparable transactions within the same industry. When I work with prospective buyers, I provide guidance, resources, and advice to help them decide on the business that best matches their requirements. To find a business for sale near you, these are the websites you can check out: BizBuySell.com, Bizquest.com, BusinessForSale.com, BusinessBroker.net, LoopNet.com, DealStream.com, and WebsiteClosers.com.

Have you heard of the ROBS strategy? ROBS stands for Rollovers as Business Start-Ups. According to the IRS, ROBS is an arrangement in which prospective business owners use their retirement funds to pay for new business start-up costs. ROBS plans are not considered an abusive tax avoidance transaction but can be questionable because they may solely benefit one individual, which is the individual who rolls over his or her existing retirement funds to the ROBS plan in a tax-free transaction. The ROBS plan uses the rollover assets to purchase the stock of a new business. Promoters aggressively market ROBS arrangements to prospective business owners. In many cases, the company will apply to IRS for a <u>favorable determination letter</u> (DL) as a way to assure its clients that IRS approves the ROBS arrangement. The IRS issues a DL based on the plan's terms meeting Internal Revenue Code requirements.

However, DLs do not give plan sponsors protection from incorrectly applying the plan's terms or from operating the plan in a discriminatory manner. When a plan sponsor administers a plan in a way that results in prohibited discrimination or engages in prohibited transactions, it can result in plan disqualification and adverse tax consequences to the plan's sponsor and its participants. If this is something that you are considering, make sure you engage a firm that can do this correctly for you. You'll need to establish a new C-Corporation in the state in which the business will be operating. The corporation will adopt a 401(k) plan which will permit participants to direct the investment of their plan accounts into a selection of investment options. You will then elect to participate in the new 401(k) plan where you can rollover your prior employer's 401(k) plan funds into the newly adopted plan. Using your 401(k), you can purchase the C-corp's newly issued stock at fair market value. The corporation will utilize the proceeds from the sale of stocks to purchase the assets for the new business. The proceeds are the amount of rollover funds and personal funds you use.

The Finance Doctor's Goals and Projects

My short-term goal is to reach out to as many people as possible with this book because I am confident that after reading and applying the concepts and techniques shared, we will reduce the 67% statistic of financially uneducated people. By reading, learning, understanding, and putting an action plan in place, people will no longer feel helpless. Instead, they will be inspired and motivated to take action towards their goal. There shouldn't be any excuse not to be successful and reach your goals. My other short-term goal is to focus on my consulting business and keep mentoring entrepreneurs because according to the Bureau of Labor Statistics, 5 out of 10 businesses will not make it to their 5th year and 7 out of 10 will not make it to their 10th.

My long-term goal is to focus on finding profitable businesses to acquire from motivated sellers and help them find the right buyers. I am a Business Intermediary/Broker in the State of Florida but can easily assist anyone needing help in 35 other states without having to get a state license. My other project in the pipeline is a portal that will change the landscape of investing.

Most of the things I've done in my business are a result of ideas from a very concentrated mind when I meditate. Remember that we cannot rely simply on our 5 senses. We should be tapping into infinite knowledge. If you're not meditating, then how will you be able to tap into the Divine

Source/Universe? If you're not reaching out to them, they will not come to you and hand things to you on a silver platter. You need to do the work. Some people think that meditation is a waste of time. My response to that is, if you're not meditating, you are losing out. When you meditate, you are able to solve problems quickly because your mind is so sharp. You don't need to spend time figuring things out because whatever download the Universe gives you, you grab it and trust that it's what you need to do. When you trust the Universe, then people, events, and circumstances will show up in your life because you are in alignment with your life's purpose.

Unfortunately, there is no short cut. You have to do the work, but half of the work is already done here for you. You are given tools in this book that will help you get to the ultimate goal, financial stability, financial security, and freedom to do whatever you want, whenever you want. But first, you have to learn to align yourself with the Universe, master your mind, and get to a position where you are always vibrating in the high frequency (500 and above). Because the Universe needs to recognize itself through you and when you are in the low vibrational frequency (less than 500), you are not in alignment. If you feel shame, guilt, hate, fear, anger, worry, pride, jealousy, vengefulness, then you are vibrating in the lower frequency. Please pause for a minute and go to the appendix and find the emotion frequencies scale.

I suggest you start observing what you say, what you do, and how you interact with others. By observing, you become aware of your negative actions and thoughts, and when that happens you know to make the shift (remember the reset button) to positive thinking. I started meditating in 2017 and I had to learn everything on my own. Be grateful that the Universe had me write this book and make things easier for you because I will break it down in detail so all you have to do is follow step by step, and next thing you know, you're getting a download of creative ideas from above.

Your Visualization

I want to spend some time on "Visualization" because this is important as I explained in the earlier chapter. After you determine your clear goal, whether it's a small or big goal, you must visualize the end result as if you already achieved it. This is very important. If you missed this one, you may not be able to achieve your goal and you will feel frustrated, then become unmotivated, and we don't want that. So how do you do this?

Have a visual in your head of what it would be like after you achieve your goals. How would that feel? Marinade yourself into that thought and allow the emotion of happiness and satisfaction to flow as if you already reached the goal. In the Law of Attraction, you attract what you are and not what you want. I can better explain this to you by giving you an example of my earlier career days with PricewaterhouseCoopers. For a senior staff accountant to be promoted to a managerial role position, he/she must act as if they are already a manager. So even though they're just senior staff, they are being trained to be a manager so upon promotion they are good to go. They are ready to perform as a manager. Does that make sense?

What I'm having you do here is the same thing. Act and feel as if you already achieved your dreams and goals because that is the best way to attract abundance. I also suggest that you create your vision board. Vision boards are great because it serves as a reminder of your dreams and goals. And if you put it in a place where you see it every day then it will help you stay inspired, motivated, and focused. Having that will help you make your ideal life a reality. Creating your vision board should be fun. It should reflect your ideal life. If you like to travel, put pictures of the places you want to go to. If you have a dream car or a house, put the pictures there. Look at old magazines and find pictures that represent your goals. If you have an amount in mind, put it there. Add your "I am" affirmation words which represent how you want to feel when you reach your goal.

CHAPTER 6
EMPOWERMENT

In the last chapter, you created your personal financial statement, so you know your net income and net worth amounts. You also determined the gap between your target goal amount and your current numbers. If the gap is huge, then you know you have a lot of work to do. So, how can you stay motivated and continue on the path of financial freedom? Stay focused. You need to keep inspiring and motivating yourself. In this Chapter, I will go over Napoleon Hill's 13 steps and then I will talk about the type of meditation I practice, and lastly, I will share my daily routine and my manifestation strategy.

Napoleon Hill's "Think and Grow Rich"

The book "Think and Grow Rich" is the result of Napoleon Hill's study of over 500 self-made millionaires. It's a condensed explanation of his Law of Success philosophy which includes these 13 principles to riches (financial, emotional, and spiritual). I suggest you read the book. Here are the 13 principles:

1. Desire: The starting point of all achievement is desire. You must have a strong and burning desire. Some people call this your "strong why". If you simply wish, that your desires will materialize, that will not bring you riches.

2. Faith: Visualization of, and belief in the attainment of desire. Through affirmations or repeated suggestions to the subconscious, you can develop the emotion of faith, which is necessary for transmuting your desires to physical or monetary equivalent.

3. Autosuggestion: The medium for influencing the subconscious mind. Because the conscious mind often acts as a barrier to sensory impressions, auto-suggestion must be used to create thought patterns conducive to translating your desires into their physical equivalent.

4. Specialized Knowledge: Personal experience or observations. If you lack the specialized knowledge necessary to build your business or attain your goals, you can supplement your own knowledge with that of other individuals.

5. Imagination: The workshop of the mind. What the mind can conceive and believe, it can achieve. The imagination is the unique faculty of humankind that shapes, forms, and gives action to desire.

6. Organized Planning: The crystallization of desire into action. To translate desire into its physical or monetary equivalent, you must form a definite, practical plan and put it into action.

7. Decision: The mastery of procrastination. Procrastination and indecisiveness are major causes of failure. Men and women of great wealth, on the other hand, share the ability to reach definitive decisions quickly and change their minds slowly.

8. Persistence: The sustained effort necessary to induce faith. Most people will throw in the towel at the first sign of opposition. However, willpower, combined with desire, is necessary to ensure that one's objectives are reached.

9. Power of the Mastermind: The driving force. Individuals can attain and apply power through the formation of a Master Mind group, an alliance of individuals with different strengths and perspectives who coordinate their knowledge and efforts to attain a definite purpose.

10. The mystery of sex transmutation. Sex transmutation entails the channeling of carnal desires and their corresponding energies into other outlets than those that are purely physical. A correlative to this principle is the importance of selecting a compatible partner.

11. The subconscious mind: The connecting link. Hill describes the subconscious mind as the intermediary between the finite mind of man and Infinite Intelligence that enables humans to tap into the forces of the Universal Mind.

12. The Brain: A broadcasting and receiving station for thought. Hill wrote, "Through the medium of the ether, in a fashion similar to that employed by the radio broadcasting principle, every human brain is capable of picking up vibrations of thought which are being released by other brains." Hill explained in this book the process by which the mind is stimulated by external vibrations and supplies a method for using emotions to increase the mind's receptivity to these sensory stimuli.

13. The Sixth Sense: The door to the temple of wisdom. The Sixth Sense refers to the faculty of the subconscious also termed the "Creative Imagination" by which humans, through no effort of their own, receive communications from Infinite Intelligence. Hill calls this principle the "apex" of his Law of Success philosophy, for it can be comprehended and applied only after mastering the first twelve principles.

To implement these 13 principles, one must prepare the mind to receive the philosophy. The first step is to study, analyze, and understand the three enemies that need to be defeated. They are indecision, doubt, and fear. Hill noted these six basic fears that usually hold humans back in their pursuit of riches are: (1) Fear of poverty, (2) Fear of criticism, (3) Fear of ill health, (4) Fear of loss of love, (5) Fear of old age, and (6) Fear of death.

So how do you overcome all these fears? For me, whenever I feel fearful, I acknowledge it without reacting to it (remember to always have an equanimous mind, because when you react to it, the more of that is what you will attract), and then, I continue to take the necessary action towards my desired goals, thus leaving no room to be fearful because my mind is focused, busy and occupied. This strategy works for me all the time.

Vipassana Meditation

Let me share with you how I got started with meditating because I always laugh when I tell this story. I came from a Christian family. In my early years, my family practiced Catholicism, so I was baptized, went through the first communion, and then confirmation. I went to a Catholic school while growing up in the Philippines, and then when my family moved to the U.S. in the 80's we went to a Protestant church. When I had my son I went back to the Catholic Church because I wanted to raise him in that environment. He went through the same religious experiences that I did. I sang in the choir while he served on Sunday Filipino mass. Shortly after he left for college is when the enlightenment process began.

After my son left for college, I contemplated the meaning of life. Then I met someone who made a huge impact on my life. Let's call him "Crazy Friend" I didn't quite understand why I was so affected by this person, but years later found out that he is my Twin Flame. I am not going to talk about that here.

I will save that for my next book (The Right Mindset,) because that's a long story. Anyway, that's how I got to start reading lots of books about spirituality, angels, metaphysical, numerology, crystals, etc. and then I was led to a MeetUp group that meets every week to meditate.

I remember driving one Saturday morning to a temple (the first time I've been to a temple). There were 2 buildings next to each other but I didn't know where to go, so as soon as I parked my car, I started walking towards the crowd and come to find out it was a different group, but I found my way to this huge open space auditorium with nothing but about 10 rows of about 20 chairs on each side of the aisle, and one chair for the teacher to sit facing the crowd. I made my way towards the empty seats in the back. Then the teacher asked that the new people sit up front, so another lady and I got up and sat in front. Then the teacher directed his attention to me and asked, "Have you meditated before?" I responded "Yes". It was downhill from there. He asked what kind of meditation I practiced, and I just started laughing because I had no idea there were different kinds. You see, boys and girls, that's why you should never lie because you will have to come up with a lie to cover the first lie. Anyway, I never went back to the place but that was a Heartfulness Meditation.

Because the Universe wanted me to learn how to meditate, another person showed up in my life. One day when we met for dinner, I told him about my "Crazy Friend" who had impacted my life in a very profound way. I told him that I wanted to help my "Crazy Friend" with his problems but I didn't know how. He advised that I tell him to go to Vipassana Meditation. He had done it before and he said it was the best gift he ever gave to himself, so I went back to my "Crazy Friend" and told him the advice. And you know what he said? "You go first then I'll go". I had every intention to help my "Crazy Friend", so instead of going on vacation to Greece that year, I ended up signing up for the 10 day Vipassana silent retreat in Georgia because that was the closest center to me.

Can you imagine not having any electronics around and not speaking to anyone for 10 days? I was so proud of myself for committing to that. I was determined to understand what this Vipassana was about and how it might help my friend, so I did everything that the meditation teacher instructed us to do. Even though I wasn't supposed to write anything down about my experiences during the course, I would sneak in my room and document my experiences because I wanted to be able to explain them to my "Crazy Friend" after the course was done.

Now I understand why they didn't want us to document anything. It's because every individuals' experience is different.

That 10-day course is indeed the best gift I ever gave to myself. Before going through the course, I couldn't even sit still for 5 minutes, but I learned to sit and meditate for 10 days straight and sit for an hour at a time without moving any parts of my body. I was so proud of myself. Anyway, after the 10-day course, we were told to continue with our practice by meditating one hour in the morning and one hour at night and then attend at least one 10-day course every year to sit and serve, but I didn't follow through until COVID 19 hit. I have to give this pandemic the credit for my stronger practice of Vipassana because the organization was so quick in organizing a group meditation zoom call every morning and every night. I had no excuse not to attend. I didn't need to drive anywhere to attend, so my practice was strengthened as a result of this pandemic.

The combination of this experience, and the books I read about spirituality, intuition, laws of the universe, etc., is how I learned to connect with the Divine/Universe and get creative ideas and download. Everything I do is divinely guided, and it is simply amazing how people and events just show up in my life to help me accelerate and get to my heart's desire. The Universe will also take people and situations in our life when we are not in alignment with them so never worry if things are not working out because it's only a temporary situation. Connect with the Divine/Universe for guidance and you'll be guided.

Looking back at the day when I was laid off from my corporate job in early 2018, I told myself that I would never work for anyone ever again and do whatever it takes to make it work. How many of you can be calm when you received news that you no longer have a job? That was my 4th layoff in my career and I was not about to wait for the 5th. I took control of my future. I knew I was capable of it. I have the credentials and experience to be an entrepreneur because I used to have a Healthcare business back in 2002. I was able to start a Home Health Agency, Nurse Staffing Agency, and school for CNA, Phlebotomy, and EKG technicians for a short period of time.

I also had my Tax Preparation business on the side while acting as the Administrator of our Healthcare business. By the way, the family business was started because my mother didn't want to see any of her daughters lose a job. That was me. I lost my job for the 1st time when I was laid off as an Arthur Andersen employee. I was working in the Internal Tax Department, so I was not part of the group that went to the other CPA firms.

The story that I like to tell everyone is that I got to deliver the two boxes of the Final Form 1065 Partnership Return and Schedule K-1's for the 2000+ Arthur Andersen partners. I remember getting the two boxes on the X-ray machine of the Chicago IRS office building because 911 just happened and security was very tight.

So, for those of you who think a college education is not necessary to succeed, I both agree and disagree. I agree that it's not necessary because there are indeed very wealthy and successful people who didn't finish college and made it big. At the same time, I think it is necessary because I feel that if I didn't have my college education, I probably wouldn't be as confident to act as the Administrator of our family business. I used to hear mom always tells us to study hard because no one will ever steal our knowledge. Maybe that's why I carry all these licenses.

Even though mom left us 16 years ago because of breast cancer (she was only 56), what she taught me carried on. One of my favorites is: "If others can, why can't I." She is why I challenge the status quo a lot. Even though I am female, Asian from a third world country, this didn't stop me from competing with highly competitive jobs. Of course, at times when it crosses my mind that I may have been discriminated against when I was laid off the 2nd, 3rd, and 4th times. One thing I know is I never felt inadequate in my education when I received the news that I no longer had a job. Mom was right. They can take my job, but no one will ever take my knowledge and education from me.

After the 4th layoff, I decided to retire from corporate work. I just allowed God/Divine/Universe/Spirit Guide/Angels to guide me, and it has been a magical and wonderful life ever since. I never worry about anything because, in my heart, I know that I am loved and everything will be taken care of, so I just focus on doing what makes me happy, which is sharing my gifts and talents with others by helping them succeed. Since 2018, I have affiliated myself with big name brand companies. I invested in myself by taking courses, getting licensed, and maintaining continuing education requirements to keep my mind sharp. How are you investing in yourself? You have to show the Universe that you're doing your part and you're getting yourself ready to receive divine gifts.

I am amazed by how people want abundance in every aspect of their lives, yet don't do anything to get there. Perhaps they don't know how. I always advise people to meditate but they say they don't have time. I honestly don't know how else one can achieve abundance in all aspects without tapping into the infinite knowledge of the Universe. We can only go by with what our 5 senses will tell us, but if we connect with the Universe, they will guide us in the right direction which is beyond our knowledge. Unless we ask the Universe to help us, they will not come to our rescue because of free will, so we have to ask for guidance. One caveat though is if what you're asking is one-sided, meaning it's only benefitting you, that means you're not ready to receive yet because, in order to receive, you have to give a lot. I mean a lot. If you want to attract love or money, that's exactly what you must give out to get yourself in alignment with your desire. Instead of wasting your time analyzing and figuring out what to do to get to your goals faster, take the time to connect to the Universe.

Let me share with you what Vipassana meditation taught me, patience, and letting go of control. These are the two things that I learned in my spiritual journey. Because of consistent practice, I can now keep an equanimous mind by being aware of my thoughts all the time. When negative thoughts come, I learned to simply observe them because reacting to them will only cause negativity, and I don't want that. This is important because we don't want to create an aversion. When I have positive or pleasant thoughts, I also make sure that I don't tip the scale too much that I crave for it. I just enjoy it while it lasts. I learned to detached myself from things and people. This doesn't mean that I don't love them; it just means that if my son caused me to feel angry, I wouldn't be reactive. I would simply go with the flow and find a way to learn from that experience. Vipassana also taught me the Law of Impermanence, which means nothing is permanent, so if you're feeling sad or you're going through challenges in life, simply knowing and understanding that the situation is not permanent will help you get through anything. If you're feeling excited and happy, enjoy that moment.

I learned that when if we spend time thinking about our past, we may feel sad because of some of the bad things that happened. Alternatively, we may also feel happy, but that happiness can turn into sadness because we can't bring back the past. I learned that when we spend time thinking about our future, we may feel anxious because of the uncertainty that life brings us. I'm sure you've seen a meme that says, "Be in the present moment." Do you even know what that means? Do you know how to be in the moment? I didn't know what that means or how to be in that state of mind prior to being an enlightened person. Now I know because I learned why we shouldn't think about the past or future as it will only put us in a negative frequency and that's not what we want.

I learned that what you're thinking at this moment will create your reality and will manifest eventually in the physical realm. That's why you have to be mindful of your thoughts and what you say about yourself because you will create more of that. I'm sure you have heard motivational speakers talk about "SHIFTING YOUR PARADIGM." That's such a big word, isn't it?

Essentially what that means is that, if you are not getting results even though you are working hard, then perhaps you should hit the pause button because you may not be going about this the right way. Think about what you need to change because what you're doing is obviously not working as it hasn't given you results, but you also have to consider that it takes time to get results so you may just need to be patient. That's why it's so important that we trust our gut feeling because it will tell us if we're not going in the right direction. If you're waking up every day miserable, then something is wrong but sometimes we don't even realize that because we are so busy and we're just on autopilot doing what we normally do. You see now why it's important to take the time and meditate and connect with the Universe and your higher self? Be obedient to the Universe and you will be blessed abundantly. Take baby steps and start with just 5 minutes of meditation until you're able to do it longer and longer each sit.

I am not telling you to practice Vipassana. I am just sharing how I got started with meditation. There are different types of meditation so try and see what resonates with you. I used different guided meditations depending on what I want to focus on. Sometimes I need help getting rid of negative thoughts about someone or something so I make a point to fix that, but the important thing is that you have to train your mind to be aware. When you're aware, you can do the next step to fix it. Got it?

Besides learning how to be patient and letting go of the control, I became more compassionate with others' selfishness, ignorance, and stupidity because when you understand that some people around you are not enlightened yet, then you know not to be at their level of thinking. What do you do? You just shake your head, smile, bless them, and walk away. That's what you do. Don't react, or else you'll have an aversion.

"The Dhamma Brothers" movie

Should you wish to learn about Vipassana, please visit the website: www.dhamma.org. As an old student, I will tell you that it is indeed the best gift you can ever give to yourself and you have no excuse not to go because (1) to attend the 10-day course or any course is of no cost to you, and (2) the centers are all located all over the world. You may ask how come it's free?

Because old students like myself benefited from the course so we decided to give back by way of a monetary donation or volunteering our time. Just like how the old students volunteered and served us when we were new students.

Have you heard of the documentary film "The Dhamma Brothers"? I suggest you watch this on YouTube or Netflix so you will understand how the Vipassana practice was utilized in the Donaldson Correctional Facility in Alabama and what the participants had to say about the technique they learned.

If you want to be the master of your own mind, you have to put in the work, but after you learn it, you'll be glad you did because you will view things in a different light. You'll be happier and at peace, because you can reconcile with people and situations in your life. It's a life-long practice.

Again, this is just my experience in meditation, so explore other types and see what type of meditation resonates with you. Just do it and learn to connect with the Divine/Universe.

The Finance Doctor's Daily Routine

I want to share what my daily routine looks like. This is my way of proving to the Universe every day that I am worthy of receiving what my heart desires. It took me a while to learn this, so be grateful, not to me, but to the Universe because you came across this book for a reason.

1. I make my bed every day because I am an organized and clean person. I believe that an organized house means an organized mind. No clutter, no noise so concentration is easy to achieve. Read Feng Shui books when you get a chance and organize your place in the most auspicious way.
2. I recite my "I AM" affirmation and say my gratitude prayer, then I meditate for one hour
3. Ten minutes of stretches, push-ups, and sit-ups.
4. Drink matcha green tea (this is good for your heart and your tummy). I do 17-hour fasting so I eat at 1p and 730p.

5. While walking my peekapoo, I pay attention to the nature that surrounds me, the trees, the sun, the air, the birds while listening to the "I AM" affirmation, feeling happy and grateful.
6. I write at least 3 things I am grateful for in my gratitude journal every day and then I look at my vision board to "visualize and feel" what it would be like when those things manifest. This is the best way to attract them fast and to get to the same frequency/vibration.
7. I set my goal for the day and prioritize my to-do list in order of importance. Working for so many years in a CPA firm, I was wired to be mindful of my time so I keep track of my time and what I do so I can look at my calendar at the end of the day and feel proud of what I accomplished. I also take frequent breaks to drink water. Drink a lot of water - it's good for your skin and internal organs. People don't realize how important it is to stay hydrated.
8. While working, I have the binaural beats in the background. Depends on how I feel, I may put the happiness beats or motivational beats, or enhancing intelligence beats on.
9. At night, I meditate for one hour, do another 10 min exercise, and walk my peekapoo.
10. The last 5 minutes before bed, I recite my "I AM" affirmation again and say my gratitude prayer then put on binaural beats, either the angelic healing choir or miracle tones, for my subconscious mind. Remember, even though you are sleeping, your subconscious mind is very much awake. This is from the Book of Job 33:15-16, "In a dream, in a vision of the night, when deep sleep falls upon men while slumbering on their beds, then he opens the ears of men and seals their instruction."

My routine helps me achieve my goals. I will tell you what I do that helps me stay sane when I am overwhelmed with responsibilities at work and home. Being the analytical person that I am, and because I'm an accountant I use spreadsheets (this is old school okay… because back then, we didn't have fancy apps as you have now). Anyway, in the spreadsheet, I put the description of the task in one column, and next to it the date as to when I need to absolutely get it done, and then I would sort the tasks in the order of importance. This is the same strategy I used when I was studying for the CPA exam. I had a test date set at the top (back then you could only take it twice a year), and then in another column I had all the dates 4 months before my test date. The next column was the subject (we were tested in 5 areas – Auditing, Business Law, Accounting Theory, Accounting Practice

Part I, and Part II), and the next column was the chapters and pages I needed to study each day. That's how organized I was. During the four months prior to the exam date, if I was not sleeping, working, or eating, I was studying. That was my life until I passed. Now, any exam I take is a piece of cake in comparison to that brutal exam. So readers, make sure you appreciate your CPA's, especially the ones who took the exam when it was still manual.

Try incorporating some or all of these into your daily routine. Try some of my strategies to get organized when you feel overwhelmed and write to me. Tell me how it transformed you because my third book will be a compilation of people and clients' stories shared with me. I want to know my readers' and clients' ways of applying techniques from this book and one-on-one coaching/mentoring sessions so people will learn from other's experiences.

The Finance Doctor's "Visualize and Feel" Manifestation Strategy

Rome was not built in a day so you have to be patient; you have to persevere. You have to be determined, you have to be clear, and you have to be very specific about what you really want to manifest. For example, if you want a relationship, be specific about the person's appearance, personality, qualities, etc. If you want wealth and prosperity, be clear on how much you want, and don't worry about HOW you're going to get it. Just think that it will happen and that you deserve the abundance in all aspects of your life. Yes, you can get everything you want! Now, use all the tools you learned and do these 10 steps.

1. BELIEVE that this strategy will work. If you're in doubt, you already lost so don't even try to proceed to the next step until you are 100% believe that this will work.

2. Write down your heart's BURNING DESIRE. It can be a relationship, health, wealth, anything you want.

3. Identify and be AWARE of your negative programming, mental blockages, lack mentality, poverty consciousness, victim mentality, and limiting beliefs about your desires.

4. CONSCIOUSLY DECIDE to release everything that is holding you back. This can be done through meditation by simply setting an intention to let go and release blockages.

5. Write down your daily habits, review them, delete the habits which are not contributing to your goal, and REPLACE them with habits that will help you transform into the best version of yourself. This may include changes in your eating, working, or sleeping habits. You may have to add new habits as well.

6. Stay in the 500+ emotional frequency all the time (see chart in the Appendix). Negative thoughts and actions will negate everything you just did above so pay attention to what you say, what you think, and what you do.

7. By now, you understand the 50 Laws of the Universe so you understand that giving back to others is a must. You must give, give, give, and give in order to take. So, unless you're giving back to others, then don't expect to get anything. If you want love, give love to others. If you want wealth, don't hold on to your money. Pay someone for the products and services you need to improve yourself. Invest in yourself. Get a nice haircut, eat only food that is good for your mind, body, and spirit, get business suits, take care of your skin and your outer appearance, continue learning and educating yourself, work with a coach or mentor to guide you, and surround yourself with only positive people. You need to wire yourself to be the person you want to become. This is very important. This is what a lot of people do not understand, and they end up disappointed. When you're disappointed, you are vibrating in a low frequency and you are moving further away from your heart desire.

8. VISUALIZE and have that mental picture in your mind of what your end-result would look like. Picture where you are, what you're wearing, what you're doing, and who are the people with you. Soak yourself into this visual and then FEEL the emotions, the joy, the happiness, and the excitement because the fruit of your labor has manifested. Your gift and the abundance from the Universe are here. FEEL that and be very GRATEFUL.

9. Take CONSISTENT ACTION towards your desired goal and pay attention to the signs, people, and events showing up in your life. They are not a coincidence, so listen to your heart and your gut. Are you seeing repeating numbers? Find out what they mean. I always see 11:11 on the clock, on the phone, on the microwave, on the text. 11:11 is a confirmation from the Universe that you're in alignment with your desires.

10. Do not obsess as to when the Universe will fulfill your request just TRUST that it will come to you and simply focus on making yourself better.

You need to consistently do the above because you want to let the Universe know that you are ready to receive the abundance and the blessings that wait for you. You see, you have to put your "end-result" picture to the "mental realm" FIRST before it can be manifested to the "physical realm". If you had bad luck last week, that's because that's what you put in your mental realm and it manifested in the physical reality. You attracted it. So what do you do to change that? Paradigm shift!. You need to change the way you think, act, and feel. You are the co-creator of your life, your situation is the result of your own action, not anyone else, so stop blaming others. Instead, decide to make that shift in your habit pattern so you can get to your end-result, your desired result, your ultimate goal.

If you have been meditating and you think you're doing everything well. but you're still not quite there yet, then go back and review the 10 steps above and see where you need to make adjustments. Maybe you still have negative patterns that you need to get rid of, but you're not aware of them yet. Be patient and always be kind to yourself knowing that in time you will get there. By the way, I did not invent any of these. You can go to the internet and read about quantum physics, emotional intelligence, spiritual knowledge, infinite intelligence, hypnotherapy, mind hacking, etc. I just merely took everything I learned and put it into a step by step to break it down for you so you'll get it. If you need more help, then go to our website to apply for one-on-one coaching/mentoring.

CHAPTER 7
THE EXECUTION

Just do it!

By now, you should have a clear goal, your financial statement completed, an action plan, and dates to accomplish each step. What is your strong determination to fulfill this goal? Write it down so you can remind yourself when you become out of focus. What would be the end-result if you accomplished it? How would you feel? Write it down.

On the other hand, if you are still not sure what to do then that simply means, you don't have a burning desire to accomplish something, so I will ask you these questions: 1. Are you waking up every day happy and enthusiastic about your day? 2. Are you now content and satisfied with your life? If not, then you are not in alignment with your higher self yet. Something is still missing, so make an intent for your Spirit Guide to help you and show you. How you got a hold of this book is not by accident, so think and meditate on it. Make a conscious decision to understand your feelings and what makes you a happy and fulfilled person. Be mindful of your thoughts and not allow negative programming, fears, and doubts to overpower you. Put an intent for the Universe to help you become the Master of your mind.

I can assure you that the strategies I shared here, not a lot of people know unless they're in the finance industry of course. Even your CPA and attorney may or may not even know some of the strategies shared here because their specialization might be different, and that changes their focus. I know this for a fact because some of the strategies I shared here, I came to know only in the last 5 years because I was more focused on Corporate Accounting, Business Compliance, and Tax Rules & Regulations.

It was my passion that drove me to where I am currently, an entrepreneur who wakes up every morning enthusiastic to conquer whatever life throws at her while helping other entrepreneurs become successful using three key principles, emotional intelligence, spiritual knowledge, and financial know-how.

Which one of these components do you need to work on? I am asking this question because that's what I want you to focus on and it better not be the Financial Know-How because I just taught you that (unless of course, you are the one who skipped all the chapters). Another good thing about learning finance is, no matter what industry you decide to be in, you have to know this. You need to know what affects your hard-earned money and use tax rules to your advantage.

Now, if you decide to pursue the Finance industry, I again want to congratulate you because the Banking and Finance industries are the ones that produced the most ultra-wealthy. I hope by now you have decided how much you want to make or what business you want to start. Remember what I taught you earlier, you must have the end result in mind. Do you want to be a 6, 8, or 10 figure-earner? Declare to the Universe what you want to make and remind yourself every day so that you only do things that will contribute to that goal.

My goal is for this book to inspire and motivate as many people as possible around the world so please help me accomplish that. When you're done reading this, don't keep it on the bookshelf. Refer back to this book from time to time. Gift a copy to a family member or friend.

The next three chapters (8, 9, and 10) are technical materials while the final chapter (11) is about our contest. If you love to travel like me, then be sure to participate. Who knows, you may get so good at manifesting your desire that you end up winning the prize. I always use my manifestation powers, and that's how I get to win prizes in raffles and contests. It's so much fun. I remember winning a TV at my last job, and then I kept winning few more times on different occasions until someone finally realized what was happening and told me that they had to take my name out of the pool to let others win. You know what's amazing, just before they would call my name, I would feel this tingling sensation from my head to toe. It's so amazing!

CHAPTER 8

LIFE INSURANCE AND ANNUITY STRATEGY

LIFE INSURANCE

It wasn't until a few years back when I learned about the different financial products and what they can do. Most of my professional career was focused on Accounting, Tax, and Compliance more than Finance. This chapter is reserved specifically for you to learn life insurance and annuity products so that you will understand what each of them can do so you can make a wise decision for you and your family.

What do you think life insurance can do besides covering your final expense and leave a legacy to your family? Are you aware that you can use a certain type of life insurance contract to fund your children's college education, their first car, their first house, their retirement, and legacy? Unbelievable isn't it? But yes, you can. Are you aware that you can rollover your qualified retirement plan like 401K or your traditional IRA to a life insurance contract and never have to worry about the required minimum distribution (RMD) and what the taxes would be upon distribution? Are you aware that you can use a certain life insurance contract to supplement your own retirement income? Are you aware that you don't have to have expensive stand-alone long term care (LTC) insurance because you can put an LTC rider on your permanent life insurance policy?

Life insurance is not only an income replacement planning tool but is also used for estate and income tax planning. If there are people in your life that are financially dependent on you, then life insurance should be high on your list. The family discussion surrounding life insurance should happen at every major event in someone's life such as when you get married, when you have a newborn, when you purchase a home, when you open a business, etc.

Death Benefits

The death benefit is the one thing that all types of life insurance contracts have in common. We buy fire insurance to protect against the risk of fire damage, we buy flood insurance to protect against the risk of flood damage, and we buy life insurance to protect our family members against the financial risk of our premature death. It is that risk that motivates most to purchase life insurance protection. There is always the possibility that a disease or accident will end our life. Any of us could become a victim of a natural disaster, an accident, or an act of violence. A long life cannot be guaranteed, even for those whose ancestors have a record of longevity and those who follow a healthy lifestyle. The risk of early death is evident to most of us, particularly when we have family obligations, dependent minor children to provide for, and unpaid debts.

Dying Early

The expenses and loss of income associated with premature death are the main reason for buying life insurance as well as the major factors in determining the overall need for it. The needs that may arise due to premature death depend upon each individual situation, such as their family structure, marital status, and financial obligations. These needs may include one-time expenses such as funeral costs, as well as a variety of continuing expenses and income needs. Some needs may be immediate and some maybe in the future. The most important family needs include the following: final expenses, readjustment income, and dependency on income needs. Examples of final expenses are doctor and hospital bills from a final illness, funeral expenses, probate, and estate settlement costs, estate taxes, federal and state taxes for large estates, mortgage loans, credit cards, and other debts, and bequests to individuals or charitable organizations. Examples of readjustment income, which is an amount provided to survivors to allow a transition from the current income level to a reduced income level are, cash for emergencies, child-care expenses for young dependent children, and preventing a reduction in the family's standard of living, due to insufficient income. Examples of dependency income needs (income required while children are dependent) are continuing family income, children's education, and retirement income for a spouse.

Non-Insurance Components

Many life insurance policies include non-insurance elements and the most common of these is the cash value. Cash value accumulation has nothing to do with mortality. A variation of the cash value element is the investment account or the variable account in policies that make use of variable returns or equity investments instead of fixed-return cash values.

This is a separate saving or investment element that has nothing to do with the insurance element in the contract. This could also be accomplished through other investments such as mutual funds. Some policies, known as participating policies, pay periodic dividends which may be taken in cash or used to accumulate additional amounts of a death benefit and/or cash value. Dividends are not insurance.

Premiums for participating policies are generally higher than for non-participating policies, and dividends are considered to be a return of the excess premium charge. But dividends have often been used as a successful sales tool because some people like the idea of getting something extra back, even though they pay more initially.

Tax-advantaged growth makes permanent life insurance an attractive wealth accumulation vehicle and source of financial protection. Conventional life insurance is appropriate when the need is primarily for the financial protection element. If wealth accumulation is part of the product's intended purpose, variable contracts offer advantages over traditional contracts. The potential for above-average returns makes variable contracts suitable for investors with long-term investment horizons.

Other Benefits

Originally, life insurance contracts only provided death benefits. Currently, many forms of life insurance include other types of benefits. Most people also buy it to protect against the risk of living longer or outliving their financial resources. Some policies have a cash value or investment features. Life insurance products may be used to protect against some of the risks or it could also be accomplished through other investment vehicles, such as stocks, bonds, and mutual funds. Unfortunately, most people save and invest too little.

Living Longer

The risk of living creates additional needs and it must be considered in the planning process. People set financial goals in life, but without a plan to reach those goals, they may never be achieved. Life insurance products and investments such as stocks, bonds, and mutual funds often play a role in helping people reach the goals associated with living. Some of the possible financial needs that may arise as a consequence of living longer include funding children's education, providing retirement income for the insured and spouse, providing a contingency fund for emergencies, building an estate value.

Some of the financial needs associated with living longer overlap with those associated with dying early, such as the need to fund education for children. If a parent dies prematurely, a life insurance death benefit can cover this need, and if the parent lives longer, the cash value in the policy will provide funds for this purpose. Providing retirement income for a spouse is another area where the needs associated with living or dying overlap. Although many people think that the greatest threat to family security would be dying too soon, living too long can create particular financial problems. Inflation may erode financial resources if retirement income benefits fail to keep up with increases in the cost of living. If a person requires medical care or assistance with daily chores and these expenses are not covered by some form of insurance, the assets that were accumulated over a lifetime may have to be used to pay the bills. Life insurance can build a contingency fund for emergencies in addition to a fund to provide retirement income.

Life Insurance as an Asset

Few people consider life insurance as a property. Is it possible for a premium payment of $200.00 to create an immediate estate or property valued at $200K? That is possible with life insurance. Here are some advantages of life insurance as property: it is an asset that is very secure, there is no managerial care, it can be purchased in any desired amount, it provides a reasonable rate of return, proceeds are payable immediately, policy owner chooses the method of payment for premiums.

Life Cycle

The human life cycle can be described in terms of three economic phases. Most people are "consumers" from birth to age twenty-two, during the growth and education phases of their lives. The work or "savings" phase runs from the end of the education phase until retirement. If a couple has children, then the "savings" phase continues until the children finish their "education" phase. At retirement, people become "consumers" again. If they wish to have an adequate amount to "consume" during retirement, people need to build a surplus during the working phase. They must consume less than they earn.

Some people also want to build large enough estates to pass on assets to their heirs, or to a charity. Others only want to build an estate big enough to live on until they die.

Single

The number of single people in the United States has increased over time. Many younger people are delaying marriage, many adults are single because of divorce, and others because of the death of their spouse. If a single person dies leaving no dependents or outstanding financial obligations, that death is not likely to create a financial problem for others. Such a person needs only a modest amount of life insurance to cover funeral expenses and uninsured medical bills. However, single people should realize that their insurance needs could change in the future, and it might be wise to purchase life insurance early in life. Premiums will be lower and insurance might be more easily available than later in life when the need might be greater. For single adults, a life policy will provide: (1) An immediate estate to pay their last expenses and any debts such as college loans. (2) Guarantee of future insurability. (3) Tax-deferred growth of cash values that may be used during retirement.

Single-Parent

The number of Single-Parent families with children under age eighteen has increased in recent years, primarily due to the large numbers of children born outside of marriage, widespread divorce and separation, and the incarceration or death of a parent. In most cases, single-parent families are headed by women. The premature death of an income earner in a single-parent family can result in financial devastation for the surviving dependent children despite the possibility of receiving Social Security survivor benefits. Therefore, the need for life insurance is great. Since death means no one remains to raise the children, single parents need to provide money for someone else to raise the children in their place and they need to provide money to pay off debts and last expenses. Unfortunately, many single-parent families have low incomes, and their ability to purchase large amounts of life insurance is limited.

Two-Income Families

Two-Income Families are prevalent today and the proportion of women in the labor force has increased dramatically over time. The reasons for two-income families range from the desire for a career, or they wish to sustain a higher standard of living, or perhaps a major purchase such as a home. In the case of married couples with children, the extra cost of raising a family, including the cost of education, is reason enough for two incomes. In two-income families with children, the premature death of either spouse can cause financial insecurity for the surviving family members because both incomes are usually needed to maintain the family's standard of living. The need for life insurance on both spouses is great to replace the lost earnings, so the family can maintain its previous standard of living.

In the case of a married working couple without children, the premature death of one spouse might not create severe financial problems for the surviving spouse. The surviving spouse is already in the labor force, childcare costs and the cost of a college education for children is not a factor. However, other concerns, such as indebtedness and current or future financial support of parents or other relatives, might prompt the need for life insurance.

"Traditional Families" are those in which only one parent (traditionally the father) is in the labor force, and the other parent (traditionally the mother) stays at home and takes care of the dependent children, and possibly dependent elders as well. Traditional families have declined in relative numbers over the last few decades. Nonetheless, the premature death of the parent in the labor force can cause great financial loss for a traditional family.

Although the surviving family members might be eligible for Social Security survivor benefits, the benefits will be inadequate to meet the family's needs. If the amount of life insurance on the deceased parent is insufficient, the family's standard of living is likely to decline. What most people don't realize is that the need for life insurance on the spouse staying at home can be equally important. The death of this spouse can result in significant expenses, such as child-care and housekeeping. Although the life insurance amounts needed might not be as high as those for the working spouse, the lack of insurance can have a negative effect on the surviving family's standard of living.

A "blended family" is one in which a divorced person with children marries someone who also has children. The premature death of a working spouse in a blended family can cause great financial difficulty for the surviving family members, and the need for life insurance is great. Both spouses might be in the labor force, and two incomes are needed to support the blended family. The premature death of one spouse may result in a reduction in the family's standard of living. In addition to children present from previous marriages, additional children may be born in the new marriage. As a result, child-care costs may be incurred over a longer period, and funds for the parents' retirement and children's college education may have to compete for limited funds. Financial planning regarding estate distribution may also be especially important for these families.

The increase in life expectancy over the last few decades has proportionately increased the number of older people in the total population. Often, an aged parent receives financial assistance or other assistance from a son or daughter. A "sandwiched family" is one in which a son or daughter with children provides financial support or other types of assistance, such as physical care, to one or both parents, leaving them "sandwiched" between the older and younger generations. The premature death of an income earner in a sandwiched family can cause enormous financial hardship to the surviving family members. The death of a caregiver can also be devastating and result in the need for thousands of dollars per year to pay for substitute care.

Juvenile Policy

An obvious advantage of a juvenile policy is coverage to pay the child's last expenses in the event of premature death. For many parents, the death of a child is not something they wish to contemplate. However, a life insurance policy on the life of a child can also protect insurability, and also offers a unique opportunity for cash value accumulation. Since the cost of insurance is lower in a child's early years, most of the premiums paid to go into cash value which grows with interest. When a child reaches college age this accumulated cash value may be used to pay the cost of education. And eventually, the cash value may be used to purchase a home or start a business.

College Planning

Life insurance purchased on a parent's life for the purpose of funding a child's college education offers several advantages over other forms of saving. Only life insurance can guarantee to complete a college saving plan in the event of the family breadwinner's death. Fortunately, it is more likely that parents will live to see their children attend college than die prematurely, in which case the policy's cash value can be borrowed or withdrawn to help cover college expenses. Tax-advantaged borrowing makes permanent life insurance a popular source of college funding. If the policy was purchased on the child's life, ownership can be assigned to the child as a gift upon graduation.

Retirement Planning

The possibility of insufficient income during retirement is another important loss exposure. Most workers retire voluntarily by age sixty-five. The major financial problem for retired workers is insufficient income. When workers retire, they lose their regular earnings. If replacement income from Social Security, private retirement plans, and personal savings is inadequate, the retired worker's previous standard of living may be reduced. The problem of insufficient income is aggravated if the retired worker lives unusually long, incurs catastrophic medical expenses, or needs long-term care in a nursing facility. Life insurance plays a well-established role in many people's retirement plans. This completes a survivor's retirement plan in the event of the insured's premature death, while insureds who live to retirement find life insurance cash values to be an important source of retirement income.

Estate Planning

Estate planning usually has two primary goals: (1) to reduce the size of the taxable estate, and (2) to pass on as much of the estate as possible to heirs. These goals can be accomplished through property transfers and the use of the unlimited marital deduction. If a family's estate is sufficiently large, however, estate taxes become unavoidable. Since the unlimited marital deduction can put off the tax liability until the death of a surviving spouse, "second-to-die" life insurance is a popular estate planning tool.

The Human Life Value Approach

The Human Life Value approach uses mathematical computation to determine how much life insurance is needed by valuing human life. The Human Life Value approach considers the human being to be an "income-producing machine. This approach determines the value today of cash that is flowing from the individual in the future. This method focuses on an individual's future stream of income. It considers such things as annual salary and expenses, years remaining until retirement, and the future value of current dollars, and translates this into an amount of insurance needed to replace the income stream in the event of premature death.

The Needs Approach

The needs approach is a method used to determine the amount of life insurance based on the survivors' needs and the amount of existing life insurance, financial assets, and expected Social Security benefits. This technique focuses on the needs of survivors, instead of the value of the insured's earnings that will be lost. It considers such things as funeral expenses, continuing family income needs, children's education, and spousal retirement income, and translates these into an amount of insurance. Under the needs approach, a family's financial needs are estimated after taking into account any Social Security survivor benefits or other benefits that might be available. The amount of existing life insurance and financial assets are then subtracted from the family's financial needs to determine the additional amount of life insurance required. A full needs analysis includes consideration of the possibility of living longer as well as that of dying early. Although a big part of the reason for identifying needs is to help determine an amount of insurance, the nature of the needs revealed will also suggest the types of life insurance which may be appropriate for satisfying these needs. Term insurance can be used to cover the needs associated with premature death, but in order to accumulate funds for retirement income, education, or emergencies, a person needs a policy that includes savings and investments.

Term and Permanent Insurance Policies

There are only two basic types of life insurance policies: term and permanent. All life insurance is a variation or combination of these two basic types.

Term life policies cover a limited time period and are pure insurance plans. If death does not occur within the policy period, the policy does not pay.

Permanent policies pay no matter when death occurs, by combining pure insurance with a financial plan. They act as insurance plans if the insured dies prior to completing a financial plan. However, the insured will accumulate savings if he/she does not die.

Term Life Insurance

Term insurance is a form of temporary life insurance coverage that may be appropriate for many families that foresee decreasing insurance needs during their lifetime. This policy provides pure protection only. These contracts cover a person's mortality risk and pay a death benefit only if the insured dies during the specified term. The term may be specified as a period of time from the inception date or as a period of time ending at a specific age. If the insured lives beyond the term period, the policy expires, and no benefits are payable. Term insurance has many practical applications for covering insurance needs and it may be combined with other elements of a person's overall financial plan. Since term insurance is temporary life insurance, the use of term insurance should be related to needs that are also temporary. The basic guideline is to cover temporary needs with term life insurance and permanent needs with permanent life. Term insurance has four basic characteristics: (1) It has temporary protection for a specified period. (2) It has no cash value or savings element. (3) Most term insurance policies are renewable and convertible. 4) The premium increase with the individual's age and are based on mortality rates. Term insurance policies may be characterized according to their renewability and convertibility provisions. It may be renewable, or convertible, or both, for a specified number of years without requiring evidence of insurability.

Term insurance has a variety of useful applications and is appropriate in three general situations: (1) When income is limited and substantial amounts of life insurance are needed. Substantial amounts of term insurance can be purchased with relatively modest annual premiums. Since it provides pure protection, it allows a person with a limited income to purchase more coverage than might otherwise be affordable. (2) To meet a temporary need. A Decreasing term policy can be used to pay off a mortgage or a loan if the insured should die while a balance remains. (3) To protect insurability and provide a person with options for the future.

The insured might wish to buy permanent insurance but might currently be unable to pay the higher premiums. He or she can purchase term insurance and convert it later into a permanent policy without evidence of insurability.

Although term insurance can play a valuable role in an insurance program, there are two major limitations: (1) Term insurance premiums increase with age and eventually reach prohibitive levels at older ages. It is not suitable for lifetime protection. (2) Term insurance policies typically do not develop cash values. Term insurance cannot be used to save money, such as saving for retirement or accumulating a fund for the children's college education. Another savings program must be set up to provide these funds.

Because term insurance protection is available at the lowest cost, it will always leave more dollars for investment. By eliminating possible over insurance or underinsurance in the financial plan results in better use of financial resources. Fixed-return cash value policies provide a low return on savings and many alternative investments (such as stocks, bonds, and mutual funds) have performed better over long periods of time. Many consumers are quite capable of managing the savings/investment side of their own financial plans.

Permanent Life Insurance

Permanent life insurance should be used for permanent needs. If a business wants to permanently retain a key employee, a whole life insurance contract is an appropriate employee benefit. Permanent life insurance would be inappropriate for covering a short-term loan, which is a temporary need. As with term life insurance, a portion of the premium is used to fund the contract if the insured dies prematurely. A second portion of the premium establishes a fund that will provide a specific benefit whether or not the insured dies. This second portion of the permanent life insurance premium makes up the policy's cash value. Permanent policies have a cash value, which comes from the difference between the cost of the insurance (what is paid for term insurance) and the amount of premium paid for the permanent policy. Accumulated values are protected and may not be forfeited. A policy may be surrendered for its cash value, or the cash value may be used to purchase another form of insurance. Policy loans are also available once a policy has accumulated cash value. However, note that the face value decreases when policy loans are made. Because of that initial difference in premium, many clients choose term insurance. But the premium for term insurance will increase as the client grows older, due to the increased likelihood of dying. Permanent policies, on the other hand, are more expensive than term policies in the early years of the policy, but in the long run, the annual premium of term insurance will usually exceed that of permanent insurance.

Types of Whole Life Policies

Most whole life policies have the same characteristics (maturity at age 100, level face amount, and cash value). Differences in whole life policies usually focus on the different approaches with respect to premium payments. There are a number of variations available in the options for whole life premium payments. Under any of these options, the whole life policy will still mature at age 100, but in some cases, the premium payment period will be shorter. For example, Life "paid-up at 65" policies require premium payments to stop at age sixty-five.

Single premium life insurance has one premium payment and lifelong coverage. In some policies, premium levels may change. Initial premiums are set at a low level and gradually increase for several years until they reach a maximum and then continue at a level amount.

<u>Continuous Premium Whole Life</u>

The most common method of payment is the continuous premium whole life policy, which is also known as a straight life policy. This is the standard whole life contract. It has all of the general characteristics of any whole life policy such as level premium, level face amount, cash value, etc., and its distinguishing feature is that premium payments are required throughout the entire life of the policy. This type of policy is often referred to as straight life insurance because it does not deviate in any way from the whole life concept. Whole life insurance is a "permanent" coverage in that it does not expire without paying benefits, either to the surviving insured or to the beneficiaries.

Whole life policies combine the protection of term insurance with a "savings" feature enabling the insured to use the policy to build economic security against the perils of untimely death and superannuation (living beyond earning years). Whole life insurance, is a contract designed to provide protection over the insured's entire lifetime. There are many types of whole life policies, but the oldest and most common type is ordinary level-premium whole life insurance or simply ordinary life.

This form of insurance is also known as "straight life," "traditional whole life," or "continuous-premium whole life."

Single-Premium Whole Life

This is simply a whole life policy with one premium payment (a lump sum amount which, together with the interest it will earn, will be sufficient to cover all future premium payments). The entire cost of this policy is paid up at the time of purchase. Except for the premium payment, a single premium whole life policy has all of the same characteristics as all other whole life policies. Single premium payment allows the policy to grow to maturity in the manner represented here.

Single premium life insurance is permanent cash value whole life insurance that is purchased with a single large premium. It requires no further premiums to keep the coverage in force for the life of the insured. Single premium whole life is the most extreme type of limited payment life where one large premium payment is made. The policy is fully paid up and no further premiums are required. Many such policies have substantial surrender charges if the policy is cashed in during the first few years. Since a substantial payment is involved, it should be viewed as an investment-oriented product.

Advantages & Disadvantages of Whole Life

The principal advantage of whole life is that it is permanent insurance and can be used to satisfy permanent needs such as the cost of the illness and burial expenses. The level premium allows the policyowner to always know exactly what the cost of insurance will be, and it offers a form of forced savings. Whole life builds a living benefit through its guaranteed cash value. The cash value can be used as an emergency fund, or cash can be accumulated for specific purposes, such as the children's college education or additional retirement income to the insured.

The major disadvantage of ordinary life insurance is that the policyowner might be substantially underinsured after purchasing the policy because ordinary life insurance premiums are generally higher than term insurance until the insured reaches a certain age. Attracted by the savings feature, some policyowners might purchase an ordinary life insurance policy and, as a result, have an insufficient amount of insurance protection.

Flexible Policies

To some, level premiums, level face amounts, and fixed benefits imply stability and safety. However, for others, these same features reflect inflexibility and missed opportunities. This is particularly true when an individual's insurance needs are changing or there are significant changes in economic conditions. In recent decades several new types of life insurance products have been developed and introduced to satisfy consumer demands for more flexibility in terms of premiums, face amounts, and investment objectives. The main types of flexible policies available include adjustable life, universal life, and variable life insurance. Flexible life insurance products provide consumers with a wider range of options than traditional policies. Although these policies provide flexibility, they also pose a degree of uncertainty and increased risk. On the investment side, there is no guarantee that these products will perform better than alternative products. On the protection side, some flexible policies do not guarantee the amount of the death benefit, so there is a risk that an insured who is seeking a better return will actually end up with less protection than is needed.

Advantages and Disadvantages of Flexible Policies

Some of the advantages of owning Flexible life insurance are: (1) The convenience of making policy changes without exchanging policies. (2) The flexibility to change the premium payment or face amount as needs change. (3) An opportunity to earn higher rates of interest than what is available under fixed return contracts. (4) Investment returns under variable policies may exceed the fixed returns under guaranteed contracts.

Some of the potential disadvantages of flexible life insurance policies are: (1) Proof of insurability may be required when an insured increases the face amount. (2) Policy changes which increase the death benefit could require substantially higher premium payments. (3) Making many policy changes could cause an insured to lose focus of the overall financial planning goals. (4) Flexible products were introduced during a period of historically high interest rates, and returns in recent years have fallen far below initial expectations. (5) The investment element in variable products is not guaranteed, and in many cases, there is no guarantee of the amount of the death benefit.

Universal Life Insurance

Universal life is permanent life insurance, it can serve the needs of individuals and businesses just as a whole life has done for many years.

Our financial climate has changed, and life insurance has had to change with it, because of the intense competition for the dollars available for investment. As inflation and interest rates increased, some financial advisors suggested that life insurance buyers purchase low-cost term insurance and put their savings where the return was better. They suggested that the client separate the protection and savings elements of a cash value policy, "Buy term and invest the difference!"

The concept of universal life insurance developed in the late 1970s from the idea that the two components of a whole life policy's death benefit, the pure protection, and the cash value-could be formally separated, giving the policyowner greater control over the funding of the cash value. Universal life policies enjoyed a surge of success during the mid-1980s when high interest rates were widely available. Sales of universal life products grew at the expense of whole life sales. Since that time, interest rates have dropped dramatically, and universal life sales have fallen while whole life sales have recovered much of their former market share.

Universal life policies are frequently sold as an investment that combines life insurance protection with savings. The policyowner has a cash value account that is credited with the premiums paid less a deduction for the cost of the insurance protection and expenses charged. The balance in the account is then credited with interest at a specified rate. If the policy is surrendered, the cash value account may be reduced by a surrender charge.

One of the potential disadvantages of universal life policies is that they may not perform as expected. When originally introduced, some companies promoted them by using long-range projections of very high interest rates (12%–to–15%). Rates have now fallen so much that actual returns will be considerably lower.

Variable Life Insurance

Variable life insurance was developed in response to the low returns earned by traditional cash value policies. The policy has two elements, death protection, and a savings/investment element. However, instead of the cash values being linked to interest rates, they are backed by equity investments and securities and are not guaranteed.

Variable life insurance is appropriate for policyowners who want some protection against inflation in the long run in their life insurance program.

Variable life insurance offers a hedge against inflation by establishing an investment account rather than a cash value account. Premiums may be fixed or flexible. Death benefits and the cash or investment value may depend upon the performance of the equity investments. This product is regulated as a life insurance product and as a security investment.

According to the Model Variable Life Insurance Regulation of the National Association of Insurance Commissioners (NAIC), variable life insurance is a policy in which the death benefit varies with the investment experience of a segregated investment account maintained by the life insurance company. Variable life insurance is not for everyone. Clients who are uncomfortable with the investment risks characteristic of variable contracts may not be suitable candidates for this product. Compared to other permanent life insurance policies, variable life policies involve some risk. In periods of falling stock and bond prices or during a recession, the variable policy presents a less desirable plan than the other types of permanent life insurance.

Variable Universal Life (VUL)

Variable Universal Life is a combination of the variable and universal life insurance concepts. The policy has elements of variable life insurance because it is backed by equity investments. The policy has elements of universal life insurance because it allows the policyowner to adjust the amount of the death benefit and/or the premium. Variable Universal Life (VUL) is similar to universal life insurance with two major exceptions. First, the cash values are not guaranteed, and there is no minimum interest rate guarantee. The cash value of the policy is determined by the investment experience of a separate account maintained by the insurance company. The second major difference is that the cash value is held in a separate account, and VUL policy owners may choose to invest their policies' cash value in any of a variety of separate or subaccounts.

Index Universal Life Insurance (IUL)

This type of insurance policy basically puts a portion of your premium payments toward annual renewable term insurance with the remainder added to the cash value of the policy after fees are deducted. On a monthly or annual basis, the cash value is credited with interest based on increases in an equity index. The gains are applied based on a participation rate that is set by the insurance company which can be anywhere from 25% to 100%. If you have this policy, make sure you know your participation percentage.

IUL is often pitched as a cash value insurance policy that benefits from the market's gains tax free without the risk of loss during a market downturn. One distinct feature of IUL is the ability for you to adjust your premium payments. As explained earlier, part of your premium payments go towards the life insurance benefit and the other portion builds cash value. If years after purchasing the policy you needed to reduce your premium payment, you can but understand that your coverage may potentially lapse sooner than it was illustrated to you at the time of your purchase so pay attention and make sure you understand.

Some of the pros of IUL are: (1) The potential for higher return due to the upside exposure to equity indexes without the risk of losses. (2) The flexibility of how much risk you'd like to take in the market, adjust death benefit amounts, and choose among a number of riders that make the policy customizable to your need. (3) You do not pay capital gains on the increase in cash value over time.

Cons of IUL are: (1) Insurance companies control the maximum participation rate and also the returns on equity indexes are often capped at certain amounts during good years (2) There are no guarantees, unlike the whole life policies which often include a guaranteed interest rate with predictable premium amounts throughout the life of the policy.

Endowment Insurance

Endowments can be perceived as forced savings plans with a death benefit. It pays the face amount of insurance to the designated beneficiary if the insured dies within a certain period. If the insured survives to the end of the period, the face amount is paid to the policyowner. From the IRS's viewpoint, endowments are not considered life insurance. Endowment insurance is seldom sold today because most endowment policies cannot meet the tax definition of life insurance. Adverse tax consequences have discouraged the sale of new endowment policies.

However, many older endowment policies are still in force, and endowment contracts are sometimes used in retirement plans. An endowment policy has the same structure and all of the same features as a whole life policy. The only difference is an earlier maturity date. An endowment contract has a level face value, level premiums, a declining amount of insurance protection, and an increasing cash value which equals the face value on the maturity date.

Endowments are purchased for various periods of time, such as 10 or 20 years, or until age 65. Because endowment policies mature at an earlier age than whole life policies, they have an accelerated rate of cash value accumulation, and the premiums for an endowment policy must be considerably higher than premiums for a whole life policy. An endowment policy will have higher cash and loan values throughout most of the policy period in comparison to a similar amount of whole life insurance.

Beneficiary Provisions

Since all life insurance policies pay a death benefit, each policy includes the beneficiary provision. The beneficiary may be a person or an institution, such as a foundation or charity. Beneficiary selection is first made in the application for life insurance. The beneficiary designation clause in the policy establishes how a beneficiary may be changed. The choice elected in the application will stay in effect unless changed by the policyowner. It is important to keep beneficiary designations up-to-date as situations change. It is also important to understand the rights associated with a beneficiary designation, and how the type of designation made may affect the payment of life insurance proceeds. If no beneficiary is living or chosen upon the death of the insured, proceeds will be paid to the owner or the owner's estate.

There are different types of beneficiary designations. A revocable beneficiary designation is one that may be changed at any time by the policy owner. Almost all life insurance beneficiary designations are revocable unless the policyowner has specifically given up the right to change the beneficiary. An irrevocable beneficiary designation is one that cannot be changed without the consent of the beneficiary. When an irrevocable designation is made, the owner has given up the future right to change designations. In the event that an irrevocable beneficiary dies before the insured, the right to select the beneficiary often reverts back to the policyowner.

Succession of Beneficiaries

A policy may provide for multiple beneficiaries as well as a succession of potential beneficiaries. Types of beneficiaries that can be designated in life insurance policies include the following: (1) The primary beneficiary is the first party entitled to receive the death benefit at the insured's death. If there is more than one primary beneficiary, they may share equally or according to some predetermined arrangement.

(2) The contingent (or secondary) beneficiary is the beneficiary who is entitled to receive the death benefit if there is no surviving primary beneficiary. (3) A tertiary beneficiary occupies the third level of a succession of beneficiaries and would be entitled to receive the proceeds only if all primary and contingent beneficiaries have died before the insured.

It is important to clearly name intended beneficiaries and to clearly state intent because careless wording of beneficiary designations can result in undesirable consequences. When the intention is not clear, the insurer must distribute the funds according to the apparent intent of the insured, or ask the court for a judicial determination of the proper distribution. Intended beneficiaries may end up without a share of the proceeds, and heirs may end up fighting in court.

Per Capita

Under a per capita ("by heads") designation, each surviving class member shares equally in the death benefit. If any class member predeceases the insured, that portion of the proceeds is forfeited to the remaining class members, who receive a greater share. No benefits are preserved for any descendants of a deceased beneficiary.

Per Stirpes

Under a per stirpes ("by stock") designation, the portion of proceeds intended for each class member is preserved for their descendants, if any. Each child, grandchild, or great-grandchild of a beneficiary moves up in place of a deceased beneficiary. If any class member predeceases the insured, that portion passes to any children or grandchildren, and the other class members would not get a greater share.

Facility of Payment Provision

Typically, this provision is found in policies with relatively small death benefits. It permits the insurance company to facilitate the payment of death proceeds by selecting a beneficiary if no beneficiary has been named or if a named beneficiary cannot be found after a reasonable time. Usually, the insurer will select someone who is in the deceased insured's immediate family (such as a spouse, parent, brother, sister, etc.) or someone who has incurred expenses for the insured's last illness or funeral.

Exclusions & Limitations

While life insurance policies generally have few exclusions, each contract is likely to include some limitations. The most common exclusions relate to aviation exposures, hazardous occupations, suicide, or war risks. A suicide clause in a life insurance policy states that the insurer will not pay the death benefit if the insured commits suicide within a certain period (usually two years) after the policy becomes effective. In some policies, suicide is excluded for only one year. The only payment the beneficiary receives, in this case, is a refund of the premiums paid less any policy loans.

Settlement options

Settlement options are available under all types of life insurance. This refers to the various ways that the policy proceeds can be paid other than a lump sum. The policy owner can elect a settlement option before the insured's death. If the policyowner has not selected a settlement option, then the Beneficiary has the right to select the method of payment after death occurs. The following optional modes of the settlement are available: lump sum (default), interest only, fixed-period installments, fixed-amount installments, Life income, Joint and survivor, and any other method approved by the insurer. Most companies will agree to distribute the proceeds under any reasonable and actuarially sound mode.

Modified Endowment Contracts (MEC)

These contracts are policies that qualify as life insurance under the statutory definition which fails to meet a 7-pay test. If at any time during the first seven years, the cumulative payment exceeds the cumulative funding limit at that point, the policy will be treated as a MEC from that point on. Once the policy is a MEC it is always a MEC. If a policy is found to be a MEC, distributions from that policy are subject to unfavorable tax rules.

Income Tax Treatment

The taxation of life insurance is not always clear-cut due to the complex ways in which life insurance may be used. Life insurance proceeds represent a great deal of money, often the bulk of an insured's estate, so tax considerations become very important. There are three unique tax advantages enjoyed by life insurance: (1) The death benefit is usually not subject to income tax.

(2) The cash value of permanent life insurance accumulates on a tax-deferred basis and is distributed income tax free if paid as part of the death benefit. (3) Borrowing or withdrawing funds from the cash value is given favorable "first in-first out" treatment.

Estate Tax Consequences

Although life insurance proceeds payable to a beneficiary are not subject to income taxes, they are frequently subject to estate taxes. This means that in all cases where the insured is also the policyowner, the benefits are included in the estate value even if payable to a beneficiary other than the estate. Due to the large estate tax exemption, the tax consequences for many middle-class families are minimal. Under federal law, a unified tax credit applies to gift and estate taxes, so estate taxes should only be a concern for those with assets greater than the federal tax credit. If the policy is transferred into an irrevocable life insurance trust (and assuming the insured has no continuing incidents of ownership in the policy), the proceeds will not be recognized as part of the decedent's estate.

1035 Exchange

Under section 1035(a) of the Internal Revenue Code, certain exchanges of insurance policies and annuities may occur as nontaxable exchange. If a policyowner exchanges a life insurance policy for another life policy with the same insured and beneficiary and a gain is realized, it will not be taxed as income under this section.

Life Insurance Underwriting

The underwriting process consists of evaluating information and resources to determine if the individual will be accepted or rejected and how he/she will be classified (standard or substandard). Once this part of the underwriting procedure is complete, the policy will be rated and the premium which the applicant will pay will be determined. An underwriter's job is to use information gathered from many sources to determine whether or not to accept a particular applicant. Life insurance underwriting is based on the basic principle of emphasizing the standard acceptable group so that most applicants are accepted at standard rates.

Important underwriting factors for individual life insurance include age, sex, build, physical condition, personal and family health history, smoking habits, involvement in hazardous sports or hobbies, personal habits and morals, country of residence, and occupation.

Group Life Insurance

In addition to individual life insurance, group life insurance is also important in providing financial security to families. Today group life insurance accounts for almost half of the total amount of life insurance in force in the United States. Group life insurance differs from individual life insurance. Many individuals can be insured under a master contract between the insurer and policyowner. An experience rating is used in larger groups to determine the premiums charged. Individual evidence of insurability is usually not required because group underwriters evaluate the overall characteristics of the group. The coverage usually provides low-cost protection to the employee. Most group term insurance plans provide an amount of insurance equal to some multiple of the employee's annual earnings, such as one or two times annual earnings. If employment is terminated, the employee has the right to convert the term insurance to an individual policy within thirty-one days with no evidence of insurability.

Many group plans also offer dependent life insurance, providing modest amounts of life insurance on the lives of the employee's dependents. Dependents include the insured's spouse, children, dependent parents, or any person for whom dependency can be proven. Generally, anyone whose coverage terminates has 31 days in which to exercise the conversion privilege. If an individual dies after the group coverage has terminated and before the end of the 31-day conversion period, the group coverage is still in effect and the specified death benefit will be paid under the group policy.

ANNUITIES

An annuity is a contract between an individual and an insurance company. The annuitant agrees to pay the insurance company a single payment or a series of payments, and the insurance company agrees to pay the annuitant an income, starting immediately or at a later date, for a specified time period. Under current tax law, money put into an annuity grows on a tax-deferred basis until the annuitant begins receiving his accumulated fund as an income. That means that one hundred percent of earnings are reinvested in an annuity and allowed to compound without having to pay taxes on earnings. There are many types of annuities. Each type is designed to meet a particular financial concern, situation, or need.

Under an annuity contract, an insurance company converts a given sum of money into a series of periodic income payments that are calculated actuarially and guaranteed to extend for a certain number of years or for the duration of an individual's life. This is the foundation upon which all annuity products exist. Like life insurance, annuities rely on the law of large numbers as well as mortality and investment experience. Annuities also protect against the loss of income. However, unlike life insurance, an annuity focuses not on how soon a person will die but on how long that person will live. Annuity payments protect against the risk that a person will live too long and outlast his or her income. They are not appropriate for short-term needs or objectives. Annuities are the only investment vehicles that can guarantee investors that they will not outlive their income, and they do this in a tax-favored manner.

History

The first modern annuity was sold in 1973. Annuity products have experienced incredible growth over the past two decades. This growth came initially from the fixed annuity business; however, in the mid-1990s, the variable annuity business really took off. Today, annuity premiums account for roughly one-third of the total income insurance companies receive. Over the past 25–30 years, the annuity has changed dramatically. It remains one of the only tax-deferred methods of accumulating long-term retirement assets. The historical definition of the annuity was to provide an income stream guaranteed for life. It is used today in a wide variety of financial planning applications to both accumulate and distribute assets earmarked for the long term.

Immediate vs. Deferred Annuities

With an immediate annuity, the insurer agrees to start making payments soon after the contract is signed. Immediate annuities are commonly used to convert a large amount, such as a lump-sum distribution from a qualified pension or profit-sharing plan, into an income stream.

Payments from deferred annuities are delayed or deferred for a period of time after the premiums or contributions have been completed. Deferred annuities are frequently used when a person has the cash to invest before retirement and wishes to postpone annuity payments until retirement or later.

Single vs. Flexible-Payment Annuities

A single-premium annuity is purchased with a single lump-sum premium payable at the inception of the contract. Generally, the contract owner is not allowed to make additional deposits into the contract. All immediate annuities must be funded by a single-premium, although not all single premium annuities are immediate. The contract holder can deposit the money into the annuity in one lump sum and let it remain there collecting interest until some time in the future when they decide to begin receiving annuity payments. Single premium annuities are ideal for people who have come into large cash sums. A single premium annuity will convert such amounts into a lifetime or certain fixed period stream of payments.

A flexible-premium annuity is purchased with periodic premiums payable on a flexible schedule. All flexible premium annuities are deferred annuities. Flexible premium annuities are used widely to fund individual retirement accounts (IRAs) and tax-sheltered annuities (TSAs). Many companies have set up preauthorized contributions to their flexible premium annuity products by systematically transferring periodic sums from contract owners' checking or savings accounts into the annuities. The duration of surrender charges tends to be somewhat longer and the charges somewhat higher.

Types of Annuities

There are three basic types of annuities: fixed, variable, and indexed with the difference based on the underlying investments. Fixed annuities are invested primarily in bonds, bond funds, or the insurer's general account. Variable annuities are invested primarily in stocks, stock funds, or stock index funds. Equity indexed products are fixed annuities tied to the rise or fall of an investment index. Fixed annuity owners appreciate stability. Fixed annuities offer assurances that cannot be found anywhere else. Variable annuities allow clients to enjoy the upside of the market but subject them to investment loss as well. Indexed annuities minimize downside risk by guaranteeing that the annuity value will earn a minimum rate of interest and that they will not decrease below the initial premium. In all three types of annuities, the earnings accumulate tax-deferred and can be used to provide lifetime income. The basic difference between fixed and variable annuities is the way each credits earnings to the contract.

Fixed Annuities

In Fixed Annuities, amounts credited to cash values are based on the insurer's current declared rate, subject to a minimum guarantee. Rates may be guaranteed for one to five years. The declared rate depends on the performance of the insurer's general investment portfolio or general account, which is largely invested in fixed-income investments such as bonds and mortgages. Similar to a savings account, once interest is credited, the cash value will not decline if the market value of the underlying assets in the insurer's general account declines. The insurer bears the market risk.

Variable Annuities

In Variable Annuities, owners bear the market risk of investment without minimum interest rate guarantees. However, they have the flexibility to choose their investment portfolio and the potential to earn far greater total returns than on fixed-rate annuities.

Equity Index Annuities

In an Equity Index Annuities, the returns on EIAs are linked to an equity index, such as the S&P 500 index. However, the annuity is not actually invested in the stocks making up the index. Like fixed annuities, the returns to EIAs are paid from the insurance company's general account. However, the amount allocated to the EIA is based on some percentage of the appreciation in the reference index, subject to annual caps. If the index declines in value, a minimum guaranteed amount is credited to the EIA. In this way, EIAs provide the upside potential of the equity markets with the downside protection of more conservative general account investments.

Parties in an Annuity Contract

There are four parties to an annuity contract, the insurer, owner, annuitant, and the beneficiary. The insurance company that issues the contract and accepts the premium. The owner is the person or the entity that purchases the contract, designates the beneficiary, and holds most of the rights under the contract. An annuitant is a natural person whose life income benefits will be based. The beneficiary is the person or entity receiving the death benefit.

Financial Stability and Ratings

An annuity policy is only as secure as the company issuing it. There are a number of independent rating services to help you evaluate an insurance company's financial strength and stability. No rating provides an absolute guarantee of continued solvency, but the ratings do offer an expert, informed opinion about a company's financial condition based on a thorough analysis of the company's circumstances. The major rating services for insurance companies are A. M. Best Company, Standard & Poor's, Moody's Investors Service, Duff & Phelps, and Weiss Research.

Annuity Riders

Insurers have developed a variety of riders adding additional features to make annuities more appealing to consumers such as life insurance rider, estate protection rider, term insurance rider, and long-term care rider, etc.

Life Insurance Riders

To help reduce the size of the income tax bill that annuity beneficiaries might face, a number of insurance companies have created specific riders that, for an additional fee, can be added to the core annuity contract. During the accumulation phase of an annuity, gains are tax-deferred. But at death, under non-qualified annuities, annuity gains are treated as income to the beneficiary and subject to income tax. The life insurance riders were designed by insurance companies to help beneficiaries offset the income tax due on annuity gains. They are especially suitable for seniors who purchase annuities with no intent to access the funds but want the proceeds passed on to children and grandchildren upon their death. If an enhanced death benefit rider is added, the death benefit can increase based on increases in the account value. Typically, this is measured by recording the highest value on any contract anniversary.

Taxation of Life Insurance Rider Benefits

Whether or not the death benefit is taxable depends on how the insurance company reports the cost of the rider. Usually, the cost of the rider is deducted from the earnings of the annuity. If the earnings deducted to cover the cost of the rider are reported annually as taxable income to the owner, the stepped-up death benefit is tax free. If the earnings to cover the cost of the rider are not reported as taxable income to the owner, the stepped-up death benefit is taxed.

A Private Letter Ruling (PLR 200022003-72.07-02) from the Internal Revenue Service defines the rules for an annuity and term life combination policy. Death benefit proceeds under the rider are taxed as life insurance and not taxed as annuity proceeds. Rider charges, to the extent extracted from the account value, are taxable distributions under the annuity policy.

Estate Protection Rider

The estate protection rider increases the contract's death benefit by a certain percentage in the event the owner dies before annuitization. The increase, which is designed to help offset the income tax payable on the contract's gain, is typically a multiple of the contract's earnings based on the owner's age at death. An additional cost for an estate protection rider applies. With a fixed annuity, this cost is absorbed by reducing the amount of current interest credited to the contract. With a variable annuity, the Mortality and Expense charge is increased.

Term Insurance Rider

As the annuity value grows, so does the amount of the tax bill due when the owner of the deferred annuity dies. Attaching a term life insurance rider to a deferred annuity helps the annuity owner pass more of the accumulated wealth to beneficiaries. Under this option, an increasing term rider is attached to the annuity contract. As the annuity credits its interest rates, some portion of the account value increases is withdrawn to apply as premiums on the ever increasing amount of term insurance. At the annuity owner's death, the beneficiary receives, tax free (or tax reduced) the death benefit from the annuity plus that from the term rider. Because the annuity's benefit is equal (or close to) to the amount of the original principal, there is no taxable gain. The term rider pays income tax free death benefits. Income taxes are payable on amounts withdrawn from the annuity to pay the insurance premiums. However, these amounts are minor compared to what beneficiaries would pay if they were to receive the traditional gain from the annuity.

The Long-Term Care (LTC) rider

The LTC rider is a popular option. According to the U.S. Census Bureau, the number of persons over age 65 is expected to double by 2030. More people together with increased costs equals a viable need for LTC coverage which LTC riders help to fill. Long-term care is a social and family issue that is becoming an increasing concern to Americans. With increased life expectancies, an aging Baby Boomer population, and a variety of socioeconomic trends, paying and providing for long-term care has become a serious problem. Seniors are increasingly aware of the need for LTC insurance. Still, paying expensive premiums for LTC insurance remains a barrier, especially when premiums become so much more expensive in the advanced years when a person may finally appreciate the need for the coverage and begin shopping for coverage. In light of this, many consumers are purchasing long-term care insurance to plan ahead for the possibility of someday needing long-term care. Annuity providers accustomed to an aging marketplace have developed annuities with long-term care insurance riders to help meet this need for LTC coverage. Many LTC riders are similarly constructed, providing coverage for catastrophic illnesses that require home health care, like an in-home nurse or aide, or long-term hospitalization, or a nursing homestay. These riders are designed to provide benefits without cutting into the monthly payments you receive from an annuitized annuity.

Annuity Taxation

Much of the retirement and estate planning focuses on the impact of taxes on the structure of the annuity contract. Annuities may be a significant part of an individual's comprehensive financial plan. There are special income tax rules that apply to annuity contracts. Clients should consult a professional tax advisor to discuss their individual tax situation.

Under current federal law, annuities receive special tax treatment. Income tax on annuities is deferred, which means they aren't taxed on the interest their money earns while it stays in the annuity. Tax-deferred accumulation isn't the same as tax free accumulation. An advantage of tax deferral is that client's tax bracket may be lower when they receive annuity income payments than during the accumulation period. They will also be earning interest on the amount that would have been paid in taxes during the accumulation period. Most states' tax laws on annuities follow federal law. The taxation of the actual annuity payments under the contract is subject to specific tax rules. In addition, such payments are typically deferred for some period of time after the inception of the contract, either until the annuitant reaches a specified age or for some period thereafter at the discretion of the contract owner. During this period of "deferral," the funds in the contract are generally permitted to accumulate on a tax-deferred basis.

However, if a withdrawal, loan, or other financial transaction involving the contract is done before the commencement of the stream of annuitized payments, additional tax rules apply to the transaction.

Qualified vs. Non-Qualified Annuities

Qualified annuities

Qualified annuities used to fund certain employee pension benefit plans (those under Internal Revenue Code Sections 401(a), 401(k), 403(b), 457 or 414), defer taxes on plan contributions as well as on interest or investment income. Within the limits set by the law, pretax dollars can be used to make payments to the annuity. When money is taken out, it will all be taxed. Annuities can also be used to fund traditional and Roth IRAs under Internal Revenue Code Section 408. If an annuity is used to fund an IRA, purchasers must receive a disclosure statement describing the tax treatment.

The term Qualified (when applied to Annuities) refers to the tax status of the source of funds used for purchasing the annuity. These are premium dollars that until now have "qualified" for IRS exemption from income taxes. The whole payment received each month from a qualified annuity is taxable as income (since income taxes have not yet been paid on these funds). Qualified annuities may either come from corporate-sponsored retirement plans (such as Defined Benefit or Defined Contribution Plans), Lump Sum distributions from such retirement plans, or from such individual retirement arrangements as IRAs, SEPs, and Section 403(b) tax-sheltered annuities, or Section 1035 annuity or life insurance exchanges.

The qualified plan market is complex. Because qualified plans are funded with contributions that use pre-tax dollars, a qualified plan must satisfy specific provisions set forth by the Internal Revenue Code. Each type of qualified plan has its own unique definitions, limitations, and exceptions. The term "tax-qualified plan" can refer to a number of different types of retirement plans that qualify for special treatment under federal income tax law.

The major tax breaks qualified plans provide are: (1) Amounts contributed to the plan are not income taxable to the individual until they are paid out of the plan. (2) Earnings in the plan are not income taxable to the individual until they are paid out of the plan. (3) If it is an employer-sponsored plan, contributions made by the employer are tax-deductible to the business.

Non-qualified annuities

Non-qualified annuities are purchased with monies in which taxes have already been paid. A part of each monthly payment is considered a return of previously taxed principal and therefore excluded from taxation. The amount excluded from taxes is calculated by an Exclusion Ratio, which appears on most annuity quotation sheets. Non-qualified annuities may be purchased by employers for situations such as deferred compensation or supplemental income programs, or by individuals investing their after-tax savings accounts or money market accounts, CD's, proceeds from the sale of a house, business, mutual funds, other investments, or from an inheritance or proceeds from a life insurance settlement.

For non-qualified annuities, part of the payments received from an annuity will be considered as a return of the premium paid. Clients won't have to pay taxes on that part. Another part of the payment is considered interest earned. They must pay taxes on the part that is considered interest when withdrawn and may also have to pay a 10% tax penalty if they withdraw the accumulation before age 59½. The Internal Revenue Code also has rules about distributions after the death of a contract holder. Annuity taxation involves the concept that the contract owner's capital investment in the contract may be recovered tax free when distributions are made. But the interest or other earnings on the contract funds must be subject to taxation at some point in time.

When to use Annuities

Some form of the annuity would be useful in the following circumstances: (1) When a tax deferred accumulation of interest is desired. The interest earned inside an annuity owned by an individual grows income tax free and is not taxed until it is withdrawn. (2) When liquidity is desired. Owners may usually withdraw cash, within limits, before the annuity starting date. (3) When an investment with immediate and high collateral value is needed. (4) When a person wants a retirement income that can never be outlived. (5) When the person would like to avoid probate and pass a large sum of money by contract to an heir to reduce the possibility of a will contest. (6) When an investor wants to be free of the responsibility of investing and managing assets. (7) As a replacement for, or an alternative to, an IRA. With less opportunity for pre-tax contributions to IRAs, many clients are seeking opportunities of making regular after-tax contributions to an investment vehicle. The annuity may be a good choice because the contribution can be much more than the IRA limitations.

(8) When a retired individual wants a monthly income equal to or higher than other conservative investments and is willing to have principal liquidated. (9) Fixed annuities should be considered when the safety of the principal is an important consideration. (10) Variable annuities should be considered when an investor wants more control over his or her investment and is willing to bear the risk associated with the investment selections

Annuity as an Accumulation Vehicle

Tax-deferral of earnings is perhaps the single greatest benefit of the annuity. Unlike other investments, such as certificates of deposits and mutual funds, the earnings in an annuity are not subject to ordinary income taxes until they are withdrawn. This gives the annuity owner control over when earnings are taxed. Income earned on the Deferred Annuity funds within the contract is not subject to current taxation. Only when funds are withdrawn are the earnings taxed. This enhances the product's ability to build assets for the long term. In exchange for tax deferral, the annuity must be used as a long-term product whose values are reserved for retirement. If funds are accessed earlier, they may be subject to a tax penalty. In the meantime, contract owners earn interest on the money they're not paying in taxes. Clients can accumulate more money over a shorter period of time, which ultimately will provide a greater income.

Annuitization Options

Whether deferred or immediate, annuities offer a variety of settlement options to help achieve different income needs. An annuity can be used to create an income stream, whether immediate or in the future. Alternatives to annuitization, including surrender and systematic withdrawals, are also available. The origin of the annuity is based on a fairly simple mathematical concept: a lump sum of money, invested today at a certain rate of interest, can be converted, or "annuitized," into a series of periodic payments, calculated to extend for a specific period of time. The basic factors are principal, interest, and time. Each periodic payment consists partly of amortized principal and partly of interest earnings. Annuities can play an important role in any situation in which a guaranteed stream of income is needed, especially during retirement. The application of the annuity principle allows individuals to enjoy their retirement years with the income they cannot outlive. This has brought peace of mind to countless numbers of investors. As longevity continues to increase and individuals begin to live 20 to 30 years (or more) past retirement, a major financial concern is a very real possibility of outliving one's assets. An annuitized income stream is guaranteed for as long as individual life addresses this concern.

Annuity Payout

An annuity payout can be structured for the duration of a person's life, a specified term of years, or a combination of both. A straight life or life-only annuity pays a benefit for the individual's life, no matter how long or short a period may be. At the annuitant's death, income ceases. A term certain annuity pays benefits for a specified period of time, such as 10, 15, or 20 years, without regard to a life contingency. A combination of life with term certain annuity pays an income for the life of the annuitant but guarantees a minimum number of monthly payments, such as 120 (10 years) or 240 (20 years).

Advantages and Disadvantages of Annuitization

The primary advantage of annuitization is a structured, guaranteed income flow for the duration of the specified period, whether it's a certain number of years or life. Each month, quarter, or year, the insurance company promises to make guaranteed payments of principal and interest to the annuitant. Especially for those in retirement, a fixed annuity payout provides a certain, known income that will not change. On the other hand, the primary disadvantage of annuitization is usually irrevocable. The contract owner cannot change the income stream during life. A fixed annuitized payout option commits the annuitant to an income flow and the methodical liquidation of his or her principal. Also, the rates of return on annuity income options are fixed at the point when the contracts annuitize and typically are not very high relative to current interest rates. Fixed annuity payouts in particular offer very little protection against inflation.

Advantages of Annuities

Tax Deferral

Because the interest on an annuity is tax deferred, an annuity paying the same rate of interest (after expenses) as a taxable investment will result in a higher effective yield. Fixed, equity-indexed and variable annuities all receive special tax treatment by the IRS, allowing earnings to be deferred until withdrawn. This is a benefit for all age groups, young and old.

For people under the age of 60, a flexible premium deferred annuity provides a systematic way to supplement employer-sponsored retirement plans where cash values accrue quicker due to tax referral. This could mean even greater tax savings if the client's tax rate decreases at retirement.

For people, 60 years and older an advantage are that annuity earnings aren't subject to income tax until withdrawn. Some investments - like CDs, mutual funds, and corporate bonds - are taxed regardless of the earnings are withdrawn. A client can "time" the receipt of income and shift it into lower bracket years. This ability to decide when to be taxed allows the annuitant to compound the advantage of deferral.

Tax-deferred funds accumulate to greater amounts over the years compared to funds on which tax must be paid each year. This is the result of what is sometimes referred to as "triple compounding." That is, interest is earned on 1. principal, 2. interest, and 3. dollars that would otherwise have been paid in taxes. Although dollars on which no tax has yet been paid will eventually be taxed when they come out of the contract, deferring taxation increases the effect of interest compounding during the period of deferral. Because of tax-deferral, annuities have a long-term growth advantage over vehicles whose earnings are taxable each year, such as bank accounts and CDs.

Annuitization

The guarantees of safety, interest rates, and lifelong income give the purchaser peace of mind and psychological security. All annuities, whether deferred or immediate, can provide a variety of income streams. Life settlement options offer income that cannot be outlived, something no other investment can offer. And if the funds are non-qualified, when annuitized, because of the exclusion ratio, the income stream is a tax advantaged as well. For younger people, annuitization can provide an income stream with the income tax on gains spread over the term of the settlement option. For older people, non-qualified settlement options may help reduce the taxation of Social Security benefits by reducing the amount of income subject to taxation.

Liquidity

Most annuities allow withdrawal of 10% -15% of the account value yearly without incurring a surrender charge. Also, crisis waivers may allow a complete withdrawal without surrender charges under specific circumstances. Because a 10% penalty tax applies when funds are withdrawn prior to age 59½, the liquidity advantage for younger people is much less advantageous than for those older than 59½. The earnings can be withdrawn instead of annuitizing, however, earnings are taxed when withdrawn. Access to at least a portion of funds provides a feeling of security in case of unforeseen financial needs arises.

Probate Avoidance

Although this is usually associated with people over 60, this advantage can apply to younger people as well. When a beneficiary has been named on the contract death benefits in an annuity do not become part of the probate estate. This allows the family access to the funds sooner and without costs of probate.

Protect cash reserve

The insurer guarantees principal, interest, and the promise that the annuity can never be outlived. This makes the annuity particularly attractive to those who have retired and require fixed monthly income and lifetime guaranteed. Principal and earnings are safe. There's flexibility through 1035 exchanges and the ability to transfer funds from one subaccount to another in variable annuities. Deferred taxation with the ability to choose when the funds will be taxed and even to spread it out over more than one generation through a stretch annuity. It's professionally managed so investors don't have to worry about day-to-day fluctuations in the market. It can be used to take care of estate taxes or other estate needs.

Surrender Charges

Surrender charges allow current owners and prospective purchasers to know exactly what the cost of surrender will be. With most other investments, the owner has no way of knowing in advance what the charge for surrender is going to be.

Another advantage of the surrender charge is that it protects the insurance company from an adverse selection in the event economic conditions might cause many policyholders to withdraw their annuities at the same time which could be catastrophic for insurers. Surrender charges protect insurers which also protects contract owners so that their funds are safe.

Disadvantages of Annuities

Possibility of Penalty

Annuities are designed to be long-term savings vehicles. With few exceptions, a deferred annuity has a penalty tax of 10% when funds are withdrawn prior to 59½. The penalty tax was created to discourage the use of annuities as short-term tax-sheltered investments. Using annuities for younger people may not be suitable. There are a few exceptions where the penalty tax does not apply. A 10 percent penalty tax is generally imposed on withdrawals of accumulated interest prior to age 59½ or disability. The 10% penalty tax does not apply for people over 59½ years old so it is not an issue for those over 60.

Annuitization

When a sum of money is annuitized, it is exchanged for an income stream. When a settlement option is selected, the policyholder relinquishes control of the deposit and once the payout starts, it cannot be stopped or changed to a different settlement option. A settlement option can't respond to the future need for additional income or access to the principal.

Tax Treatment of Gains

Receipt of a lump sum at retirement could result in a significant tax burden. Annuity gains are taxed as ordinary income when they are distributed. If a settlement option is elected, gains are generally spread over the duration of the settlement option. Annuity gains are not treated as capital gains. Under current tax laws, the top ordinary income tax rate is 37% while the top capital gains rate is 20%. For younger people, this is not a significant issue because the pre-59½ penalty tax is designed to discourage access for younger people anyway while an annuity is in a state of tax deferral. However, older people in high tax brackets should compare annuities with other income options that may be available. A long-term cash flow stream of a fixed amount may not keep pace with inflation. With a few limited exceptions, an annuity contract held by a corporation or other entity that is not a natural person is not treated as an annuity contract for federal income tax purposes. This means that income on the contract each year is treated as current taxable ordinary income to the owner regardless of whether or not withdrawals are made.

Surrender Charges

If the client is forced to liquidate the investment in the early years of an annuity, surrender charges could prove expensive to compensate the insurer for the sales charges and other expenses. If annuities are liquidated prior to their term, surrender charges usually apply. Some annuity contracts have excessively high surrender charges. For older people who may need access sooner than younger people, surrender charges can be a huge disadvantage. Some products have surrender charges that last many years. Annuity contracts are available with surrender charges as short as three years.

Annuities in comparison with Other Investments

Certificate of Deposit

Like annuities, CDs are not tax free. The principal is protected and free of market risk, a charge applies to early withdrawals, and there is limited liquidity. Unlike annuities, CDs are not tax deferred, there is no 10% tax penalty for pre 59½ distributions, there is no provision for a tax-advantaged lifetime income. The CD does not avoid probate and it cannot help reduce the taxation of social security.

Money Markets

Like annuities, money market accounts are free from market risk and principal risk and neither investment is tax free. Unlike annuities, there is no tax penalty for early distribution nor is there a fee. Money market accounts have more liquidity than annuities but do not offer any provision for tax-advantaged lifetime income or avoid probate or help reduce tax on social security benefits.

Mutual Funds

Neither annuities nor mutual funds are tax free investments. Unlike annuities, mutual funds are not tax deferred, they do not provide protection from either market or principal risk. There is no fee for early withdrawal nor is there a tax penalty for pre 59½ distributions. Mutual funds do provide more liquidity but they do not provide tax-advantaged lifetime income, avoid probate, or help to reduce taxation of social security benefits.

Stocks

Neither stocks nor annuities are tax free. Unlike annuities, stocks are not tax-deferred. Stocks are subject to both market risk and principal risk. Stocks allow more liquidity than annuities. There is no fee for early withdrawals nor is there any tax penalty. Stocks do not avoid probate nor do they help reduce tax on social security benefits.

Bonds

Bonds have about the same amount of liquidity as annuities. Unlike annuities, bonds are not free from market risk, and with the exception of government bonds, they are also subject to principal risk. Most bonds do not contain a charge for early withdrawal and are not subject to the 10% tax penalty for pre-age 59½ withdrawals either. Bonds do not provide a tax advantaged lifetime income nor do they avoid probate or help reduce taxation on social security benefits.

Commodities

Neither annuities nor commodities are tax free investments. Both allow access to investments; however, the commodities do not charge a fee for access nor a tax penalty for early withdrawal. Unlike annuities, commodities do not provide a tax advantaged lifetime income nor do they avoid probate or help reduce taxation of social security benefits.

Options

Both options and annuities allow access to funds and neither is a tax free investment. Unlike annuities, options are not tax-deferred.

They are subject to both market risk and principal risk. Options may charge a fee for early withdrawals but are not subject to the 10% tax penalty for pre-age 59½ withdrawals. Options don't provide a tax advantaged lifetime income nor do they avoid probate or help to reduce tax on social security benefits.

Limited Partnerships

Neither limited partnerships nor annuities are tax free investments. Unlike annuities, limited partnerships are not tax deferred. The principal is free from market risk however they don't provide safety of the principal. There is no access to the account value therefore there is no penalty tax on pre 59% withdrawals. There is no provision for tax-advantaged or lifetime income. They don't avoid probate nor do they reduce taxation of social security benefits.

Promissory Notes

Like annuities, promissory notes provide the safety of the principal. Neither promissory notes nor annuities are tax free investments. Unlike annuities, promissory notes are not tax deferred. The principal is not free from market risk. No access to the account value therefore there is no penalty tax on pre-age 59½ distributions.

Promissory Notes do not provide tax-advantaged lifetime income. They do not avoid probate and do not reduce the taxation of social security benefits.

Real Estate Investment Trusts (REITs)

Like annuities, there is access to the account value. Neither REITs nor annuities are tax free. Unlike annuities, REITs are not tax deferred and the principal is not free from market risk. REITs do not provide safety of principal nor do they charge for early withdrawal. There is no 10% penalty for pre-age 59½ distributions. REITs do not provide tax-advantaged lifetime income. They do not avoid probate nor do they reduce taxation of social security benefits.

Viatical Settlements

Like annuities, viatical settlements are free from market risk. Neither viatical settlements nor annuities are tax free. Unlike annuities, viatical settlements are not tax deferred. They do not provide the safety of the principal. They do not allow access to the account value nor do they apply a penalty for pre-age 59½ distributions. There is no tax-advantaged lifetime income. Viatical Settlements don't avoid probate nor do they reduce taxation of social security benefits.

Savings

Like annuities, savings are free from market risk and principal risk and neither investment is tax free. Unlike annuities, there is no tax penalty for early distribution nor is there a fee. Savings accounts have more liquidity than annuities but do not offer any provision for tax-advantaged lifetime income or avoid probate or help reduce tax on social security benefits.

Annuity Investing Advantages

There is no such thing as the perfect investment, however, an annuity provides more features than any other type of investment available, including safety, reserves, financial strength, and ratings.

Safety

By all investment standards, the fixed-rate annuity investment is unequaled. In a fixed-rate annuity, the principal is guaranteed every single day. In addition, the contract owner is permitted to terminate the contract at any time—after a day, month, or year. In addition to the principal guarantee, the interest rate also is guaranteed. The interest rate is guaranteed for a specific period of time, depending on the contract. Variable annuities are less safe because the investor decides the type of portfolio to enter into and the dollar amount that is going to be invested.

Reserves

Banks must, by law, set aside a certain amount into reserves for every dollar deposited into the bank. That amount can range from zero cents to ten cents on the dollar. When a fixed-rate annuity is purchased, the insurance company must also, by law, set aside reserves. The insurance company can use the reserves for settling withdrawals and redeeming annuities. The insurance company's reserve money cannot be used to pay claims, overhead, bad debts, or any other nonrelated annuity items. The insurance company accumulates the money to put into the reserve from other profit centers. As a rule, the insurance carriers' annuity business represents the smallest source of its revenue and the money can be obtained from the carrier selling life insurance and other forms of insurance. Most states now require that the insurance company become part of the legal reserve pool. This pool protects the investor. Should an insurance company go out of business, the reserve pool operates in a straightforward manner and the remaining insurance companies must reserve the liabilities and the obligations of the carrier that went out of business.

Financial Strength

There are more than 2,000 life insurance companies in the United States, and they collectively own, manage, or control more assets than all the banks in the world combined. Collectively they own, manage, or control more assets than all of the oil companies in the world combined. During the Depression, the insurance companies, not the federal government, bailed out the banking industry.

Ratings

Annuities have a perfect track record, but consideration should be given to the insurance company providing the annuity. Some companies are safer than others. The oldest rating company in the country is A.M. Best. They rate companies in the following manner: A+ (superior rating), A (excellent rating), A- (excellent rating also), B+ (very good), B (good), C+ (fairly good), and C (fair). Most investors prefer to stick with the A+ or A-rated companies for fixed-rate annuities. For variable annuities, the rating of the insurance carrier is of little importance because the earnings are not tied to the solvency of the insurer.

Professional Management

Professional management plays a very important role in the annuity field. The investment team or professional manager that oversees an annuity portfolio is in fact a specialist. These individuals are highly skilled and trained to focus on a certain segment of the marketplace.

There are several independent sources that track the performance of fixed-rate and variable annuities. Some of these rating services are Morningstar, Lipper Analytical Services, VARDS, and Standard & Poor's. In addition, The Wall Street Journal and Barron's published articles from time to time related to annuities and annuity performance.

Avoidance of Probate

When an individual dies, the value of the following becomes part of the decedent's estate: Assets, Real Estate, Bank Accounts, Boats, Stocks, Vehicles, Arts, Jewelries, etc. Probate fees are based on the gross value of the estate. This fee may be much higher than anticipated since the value of the estate will increase between now and the individual's death, and the lawyer who probates the estate may ask the court for additional fees. The value of an annuity will not be included when the gross estate is valued because all annuities avoid probate.

Financial Concerns

A generation ago, Social Security and pensions took care of most people's needs during retirement, which lasted an average of only twelve years. With people retiring earlier and living longer, many may spend almost as much time in retirement as they did in the workforce. Traditionally, the American retirement savings system has rested on three legs: Social Security, employer pensions, and personal savings. But with Social Security and conventional defined benefit pension plans predicted to play a considerably smaller role in providing retirement income in the future, it is clear that individuals must take a more active role in providing for their own retirement security.

According to the Social Security Administration, Social Security currently protects 150 million workers with over 44 million people receiving retirement, survivor, and disability benefits. Social Security was never intended to provide full retirement income for working Americans. Instead, it was designed to complement other sources of retirement savings, such as pensions. Social Security is funded by a combination of employee deductions and employer matching funds (or self-employment contributions) up to a maximum taxable earnings limit. Most currently working adults will qualify for benefits with 40 credits (10 working years). Special rules apply to access benefits for survivors and to access disability benefits provided under Social Security. Social Security benefits are an important income source for retirement, but they are not enough. No one knows what the future of Social Security will be.

When Social Security started in 1935, a 65-year-old had an average additional life expectancy of just over 12 years; today that figure is over 17 years and rising. By 2030, there will be almost twice as many older Americans as there were in 2000. At the same time, the number of workers paying into the system per beneficiary will shrink. Many people think Social Security tax contributions are held in interest-bearing accounts earmarked for payments to future retirees. Social Security is a "pay-as-you-go" system, which means taxes paid by today's workers' fund benefits for today's retirees. Social Security is now taking in more taxes than it pays out in benefits, with excess funds credited to the Social Security's trust fund.

By 2040, individuals who reach age 65 are projected to live until age 81 to 85 for men and age 84 to 88 for women, according to the National Center for Health Statistics. This is primarily a result of improved health care, both in the form of preventative medicine and during the later years of life. Medical advances allow older Americans to remain active. Healthier lifestyles are also a contributing factor.

Estate Planning

Estate planning involves the orderly process of transferring wealth from one generation to another with as little loss due to taxes, probate, and other costs as possible so that the maximum amount is passed on per the deceased's wishes. A good estate plan must be reviewed and updated as life situations change. If a premature death should occur, the accumulating funds within the annuity may be transferred to named beneficiaries, avoiding the expense, delay, frustration, and publicity of the probate process. Like most assets, the annuity is part of the taxable estate, but since they pass to beneficiaries without a probate, the money is available to them almost immediately after death. An important part of estate and financial planning is dealing with disability or incapacity. Durable powers of attorney, medical powers of attorney, living wills, and health care directives should be drawn up by competent legal professionals so that the senior's wishes can be carried out even if they are mentally or physically unable to do so themselves. Another important element of estate planning is to address whether the estate will be subject to estate taxation.

If it is anticipated that the estate will be taxable, it may be possible to establish trusts or charitable giving arrangements that will minimize the taxes paid on the estate, often through the use of annuities. Life Insurance riders can also help by providing funds to pay estate taxes.

CHAPTER 9
GENERAL SECURITIES

I'm dedicating this chapter solely to General Securities to share some of the fundamental concepts without overwhelming you. This is not an easy topic to comprehend but I want to introduce you to some of the terminologies. The information here is from the course materials when I took the Series 7 exam last year.

INVESTMENT RISKS

Systematic (Non-Diversifiable) Risk

Systematic risk is caused by factors that affect the prices of virtually all securities. Interest rates, recession, and wars all represent sources of systematic risk since they affect all securities markets to some degree and cannot be avoided through diversification. The following are different types of systematic risk:

1. Market risk represents the day-to-day potential for an investor to experience losses due to market fluctuations in securities' prices. Any security being bought and sold can decline as it's traded in the market. In a prolonged bear market, most stocks will trade down regardless of the company's individual prospects.

2. Interest-Rate Risk As mentioned in Fundamentals of Debt, interest-rate risk primarily affects existing bondholders, since the market value of their investments will decline if interest rates rise.

3. Inflation (purchasing-power) risk is experienced by investments that provide fixed payments (e.g., bonds and fixed annuities). Inflation is the rising price levels of goods and services as measured by the Consumer Price Index (CPI). Ultimately, inflation diminishes the real value of a dollar by decreasing its purchasing power.

4. Event risk is the risk that a significant event will cause a substantial decline in the market value of all securities (e.g., the 9/11 terrorist attack).

Unsystematic (Diversifiable) Risk

In contrast to systematic risk, unsystematic risk is based on circumstances that are unique to specific security and may be managed by diversifying the assets in a portfolio (i.e., by selecting stocks possessing different risk-return characteristics). The following are different types of unsystematic risk:

1. Business risk is the risk that certain circumstances or factors may have a negative impact on the operation or profitability of a specific company. For example, a company's prospects may suffer due to either increased competition or decreased demand for its goods or services.

2. Regulatory risk is the risk that regulatory changes may have a negative impact on an investment's value. For example, an FDA announcement denying approval of a new drug may cause the price of a pharmaceutical company's stock to decline.

3. Legislative risk is the risk that new laws may have a negative impact on an investment's value. Changes in the law can occur at any level of government and can potentially affect all sorts of investments. For example, an increase in the legal drinking age could hurt the sales of a beer producer.

4. Political risk is simply defined as the risk that foreign investors will lose money due to changes that occur in a country's government or regulatory environment. This risk is typically associated with emerging markets countries and may include acts of war, terrorism, and military coups.

5. Liquidity risk is the risk that investors may be unable to dispose of a securities position quickly and at a price that's reasonably related to recent transactions. This type of risk tends to increase as the amount of trading in a particular security decreases.

6. Opportunity cost or opportunity risk represents the possibility that the return of a selected investment is lower than another investment that was not chosen. For example, an investor may be planning to hold a bond until maturity and is therefore unconcerned with the potential decline in its price if interest rates rise.

7. Reinvestment risk is the risk that an investor will not be able to reinvest her principal at the same interest rate after a bond matures or is called. This situation typically occurs when interest rates have fallen.

8. Currency or exchange-rate risk is the possibility that foreign investments will be worthless in the future due to changes in exchange rates.

9. Capital risk is the risk that an investor could lose all or a portion of her investment. Purchasers of options are significantly impacted by capital risk because, if the options purchased expire worthless, the investor will lose 100% of his capital.

10. Credit risk or default risk is the risk that a bond issuer will not make payments as promised. U.S Treasuries are assumed to have virtually no credit (default) risk. The rating companies that were described in an earlier chapter provide information to market participants concerning the credit risk of an issuer's bond offering.

11. Call risk is the risk that an issuer may decide to pay back its bondholders prior to maturity. Bonds are typically called when interest rates fall; therefore, bondholders receive their money back early and are unable to earn the same return when searching for a replacement investment.

12. Prepayment Risk. In addition to the risks inherent in all fixed-income investments (e.g., interest rate, credit, and liquidity risk), mortgage-backed securities are subject to a special type of risk that's referred to as prepayment risk. This risk is tied to homeowners paying off their mortgages early. When interest rates fall, homeowners have an incentive to refinance and pay off their existing mortgages.

FUNDAMENTAL ANALYSIS

Fundamental analysis focuses on analyzing individual companies and their industry groups. Important items for a fundamental analyst include a company's financial statements (e.g., its balance sheet and income statement), details regarding the company's product line, the experience and expertise of the company's management, and the outlook for the company's industry. Obviously, the general condition of the economy will also affect the prospects of a given company.

Conversely, technical analysis focuses on market sentiment or trading trends. Investors who subscribe to technical analysis tend to be more short-term oriented and may even attempt to time markets as a security fluctuates in value.

Balance Sheet

A corporations' balance sheet (also called a statement of financial condition) represents the financial picture of a company as of a specific date. The balance sheet is divided into three major sections - Assets, Liabilities, and Stockholders' Equity. The name balance sheet is derived from the fact that the total assets must always equal the sum of the total liabilities plus the stockholders' equity. Assets represent all of the items that are owned by a corporation, while the liabilities section contains all of the items that are owed by the corporation. The difference between a corporation's total assets and its total liabilities is stockholders' equity (also referred to as net worth). There are three basic subsections to the asset category: current assets, fixed assets, and intangible assets.

The Asset Section

Current assets represent cash and other items that may be converted into cash within a short period. The assets that may be converted into cash include marketable securities, accounts receivable, and inventories. It is important to examine the method being used for valuing the inventory. In most cases, either the LIFO (last-in, first-out) or FIFO (first-in, first-out) method is used. Using LIFO, the cost of the last item produced is applied to the price of the first item sold from inventory. The FIFO method applies the cost of the first item produced to the money received from the first item sold. In a period of rising prices, FIFO results in greater earnings before interest expense and taxes (EBIT) because a lower cost basis is used for the units that are being sold. Therefore, the company would report greater profits and pay a greater amount of taxes. If LIFO is used during an inflationary period, it results in lower profits and taxes.

Fixed Assets are items that are used by the company in its day-to-day operations to create its products. This section will list the company's physical property, such as land, buildings, equipment, and furniture. With the exception of land, fixed assets lose some of their value each year due to normal use. The IRS allows a company to claim this wear and tear on assets as a depreciation deduction against income. On the balance sheet, fixed assets are shown at a value that represents their original cost less accumulated depreciation.

Intangible Assets. Although intangible assets don't have physical value, they add substantial value to a company. Some intangible assets differentiate the company from its competitors and are proprietary such as patents, intellectual property, trademarks, franchises, and copyrights. Goodwill is another intangible asset that's created when a company buys or merges with another company. It represents the amount that was paid above the fair market value to acquire a company.

The Liabilities Section

The liabilities section identifies the company's debts. Some of the debts must be paid in a short period (current liabilities), while others are not required to be repaid for many years (long-term liabilities).

<u>Current Liabilities</u> are debts that become due in less than one year and are easily identified by the word payable. Included in this section are accounts payable (the amount a company owes for goods and services that are purchased on credit), dividends payable, interest payable, notes payable, and taxes payable.

<u>Long-term liabilities</u> are debts incurred by a corporation that becomes payable in one year or more, such as bonds and long-term bank loans.

The Stockholders' Equity section

The stockholders' equity section represents the company's net worth and also indicates the shareholders' ownership interest. The items listed in this section include the different classes of stock, retained earnings, and capital surplus.

Income Statement

The other significant financial document used in fundamental analysis is the income statement—also called the profit and loss statement. The income statement shows a company's financial performance during a specified period and provides detailed information about the company's revenues and expenses. If revenues exceed expenses, the difference represents the company's net income. However, if expenses exceed revenues, the result for the company is a net loss.

<u>Sales</u> (revenues) represent the total money received and the amounts billed (although not yet collected) from the company's primary source of business. Sales are reduced by day-to-day operating expenses to arrive at operating income.

<u>Operating expenses</u> reflect the daily costs of doing business and include the amount claimed for the depreciation of fixed assets. There are two ways of accounting for depreciation expenses; straight-line and accelerated.

Straight-line depreciation produces a constant depreciation expense and a constant decline in the carrying value of an asset. On the other hand, accelerated depreciation allows for a faster rate of decline in the value of an asset in the early years of ownership, leading to a greater depreciation charge.

Operating income is adjusted for other forms of income (or expenses) that are not generated by normal operations, leaving earnings before interest expense and taxes (EBIT). Other income usually represents income generated by investments (dividends and interest). However, other income may also reflect extraordinary items, such as earnings from the sale of assets or losses incurred by discontinuing a part of the business.

Earnings Before Interest, Taxes, Depreciation, and Amortization (EBITDA) Margin

EBITDA may be used to analyze the profitability between companies and industries by eliminating the effects of bonds and accounting decisions (e.g. depreciation) which allows for comparisons between companies. EBITDA represents the earnings of a company before the deduction of interest expenses, taxes, depreciation, and amortization.

EQUITIES

Many businesses are organized as corporations. As a legal entity, a corporation may legitimately do many of the same things that a natural person is able to do. For example, it may buy property, obtain loans, sue, and be sued. Although a corporation is owned by its shareholders, the business is considered a separate person under the law and, therefore, an individual shareholder generally is not held personally responsible for the corporation's debts. If a business fails, the most a shareholder may lose is her original investment—this feature is referred to as limited liability.

Corporate Organization

Corporations vary greatly in both size and complexity—ranging from enormous international conglomerates to small family businesses. However, the basic structure remains the same. The shareholders of the company elect a board of directors who are responsible for overseeing the company. The board of directors, in turn, appoints the company's senior managers who run the company. In many cases, certain senior executives of the corporation, such as the CEO and the president, also serve on the board of directors. These persons are referred to as affiliated directors. Non-affiliated directors (outside directors) are the persons who are not otherwise connected to the corporation.

In small corporations, a limited group of people often owns all of the stock and also serves as the corporation's directors and managers. Since there is no public market for the stock of these companies, these corporations are referred to as closed or privately held.

Raising Capital

It's inevitable that at some point a corporation may need to raise additional capital to fund its operations. There are two basic methods used by corporations to raise money—debt financing and equity financing. When an issuer sells bonds (debt), it's borrowing money from the investors who buy the bonds. The funds are borrowed for a predetermined period with interest being paid over the course of the loan. Bondholders have no ownership interest in the corporation and no influence in its management. For bond investors, their returns are limited to the interest that the corporation pays them for the use of their money.

Another way for a corporation to raise money is to issue stock. In contrast to bondholders, investors who purchase stock become part owners of the corporation. Since the investors are provided with an ownership interest in the corporation, these instruments are referred to as equity securities. Unlike when bonds are issued, the corporation is not required to pay interest on these equity securities and there's no maturity date.

So what is the upside for equity investors? If a company prospers, shareholders can expect to share in its profits in the form of cash or stock distributions (dividends) and an increase in the value of their shares. However, if a company fails, shareholders are more likely than other investors to lose their entire investment. This is due to the fact that bondholders and other creditors have a higher claim against the company's assets at liquidation

Common Stock

Common stock is (1) the basic unit of corporate ownership, (2) the most widely issued type of stock, and (3) the first type of stock that a corporation issues. For bookkeeping purposes, common stock is usually issued with a par value that's a nominal amount used for the company's financial statement. There is no relationship between the par value of equity security and its market value.

Preferred Stock

Preferred stock is usually issued by established companies that already have common stock outstanding. These shares are suitable for investors who are more interested in income than capital appreciation—the same type of investors who might otherwise purchase bonds. Remember though, preferred stockholders don't usually have voting rights. Preferred stock is normally issued with a par value of $100, which corresponds to its initial market price, and carries a specified dividend.

Derivative Securities

Derivative securities are special types of investments that track the value of common stock or some other underlying asset. For example, imagine security that provides the owner with the opportunity to buy 100 shares of IBM at $105 per share regardless of how high the stock may rise in the near future. This is the position in which the buyer of a call option will find himself. If IBM rises above $105, the call option has value since the investor is entitled to buy the shares at a price below the current market price. On the other hand, if IBM declines in value to below $105, the call option would have little value since the stock could be purchased in the market at a better price than what is available with the call option. There are three types of derivatives—rights, warrants, and options.

Preemptive Rights

An exclusive privilege of common stockholders is that they may be entitled to preemptive rights. When a corporation intends to issue additional shares of stock, a rights offering may be conducted to provide current shareholders with the opportunity to buy the shares before they are offered to the public. In doing so, the current shareholders are able to maintain their proportionate ownership interest in the company.

If shareholders choose not to subscribe to the offering, their percentage of ownership and ability to control the company's future will be diluted by the new stock offering.

Warrants

A warrant is another type of equity security that may be issued by corporations. Like rights, warrants give the holder the ability to buy the issuer's common stock at a specified price (the subscription price) in the future.

However, unlike stock rights that have a relatively short life, warrants have a maturity that's often set years in the future. In fact, some warrants have a perpetual (endless) life.

Tax Issues Associated with Equity Securities

There are two issues that are of primary concern, (1) the tax status of the securities' periodic dividend payments, and (2) the resulting capital event at the time of resale.

Dividends—Cash Dividends

Dividends may be paid in the form of cash or additional shares of stock. Cash dividends are taxable in the year in which they are received by the shareholder. Individuals must pay tax on the full amount of all cash dividends received, even if those dividends are subsequently reinvested with the issuer.

Corporate Dividend Exclusion

Corporations are given preferential tax treatment on any dividends that they receive from other corporations. The corporate exclusion is available for cash dividends paid on common and preferred stock. In general, if a corporation owns less than 20% of the distributing corporation, 50% of the dividend income will be excluded from corporate income. If the corporation owns 20% or more of the distributing corporation, the exclusion is 65% of the total dividends received.

Stock Dividends

Stock dividends are not taxable at the time of receipt because, although the shareholder is receiving more shares, they will have a reduced basis per-share. With stock dividends, the taxable event occurs when the acquired shares are eventually sold.

Stock Splits

For tax purposes, stock splits and stock dividends receive the same tax treatment. The shares received from either action are not taxable at the time of receipt. The only action required is for the investor to adjust his per-share cost basis in the security. A gain or loss will result from any subsequent sale of the shares.

Again, with a forward stock split, the number of shares owned will increase and the cost basis per share will decrease. With a reverse stock split, the number of shares owned will decrease and the cost basis per share will increase.

Rights Offerings

When a corporation sells additional shares of stock through a rights offering, it will distribute stock rights to its shareholders. As with stock dividends and stock splits, rights are not immediately taxable, but will instead be used in calculating the cost basis of any stock purchased through the offering. However, if the shareholder were to sell his rights in the open market, the proceeds would be taxable as ordinary income.

Cost Basis of Securities

The cost basis of a security is the total price paid to acquire the security including any transaction costs (e.g., commissions). If Mr. Smith purchased 100 shares of ABC at a cost of $10 per share, his cost basis will be $1,000. As explained previously, his cost basis will be adjusted proportionately for stock splits or stock dividends. For tax purposes, an investor's profit or loss is calculated based on the difference between the cost basis and the proceeds from the sale.

Capital Gains and Losses

Recognition of Gains and Losses Securities such as stocks, bonds, and options are considered capital assets. For an investor, any sale of these assets will likely produce either a capital gain or capital loss. These gains or losses are typically recognized in the year in which the asset was sold. If a capital asset is sold for more than its cost, it's considered a capital gain. On the other hand, if a capital asset is sold for less than its cost, the result is considered a capital loss. When the holding period for the asset exceeds one year, the gain or loss is considered long-term. However, if the holding period for the asset is one year or less prior to its sale, any gain or loss is considered short-term. Whether a capital gain is classified as short-term or long-term may have significant tax implications for investors. Due to tax law changes enacted in 2013, long-term capital gains are taxed at a maximum rate of 20%, while short-term capital gains are taxed at the same rate as ordinary income. Any gains or losses that are generated from short sales are typically treated as short-term capital gains or losses since a holding period for the security is not established.

Wash Sale

The IRS does not allow an investor to claim a deduction for a capital loss on an investment if he purchases "substantially the same security" within 30 days of the sale. The period covered by the wash sale rule is actually 61 days since it includes the date of sale and 30 days both before and after the date of sale. If a security is sold for a loss, the seller must wait a minimum of 31 days before repurchasing the same or similar security. If a wash sale is determined to have occurred, the loss is denied and will be added to the cost basis of the new purchase.

DEBT

As described earlier, there are two methods a corporation may use to raise capital through the sale of securities—issuing bonds and issuing stock. Many large corporations use both methods to finance their operations. Unlike investors who buy stock, bond investors don't become part owners of the company; instead, they become creditors.

Bond Characteristics

A bond is a contract between an issuer and an investor. As stated previously, the investor lends money to the issuer and the issuer (the debtor) promises to repay debt service. Debt service represents the total of all of the interest payments over the bond's life and the bond's par value at maturity. The issuer must stand ready to make payments since, if any payments are missed, it's considered to be in default. For an issuer, raising capital through debt is referred to as leverage financing since the issuer is borrowing against its net worth. Actually, when a corporation has more debt than equity outstanding, it's considered a leveraged issuer.

Bond Pricing

A bond's price is usually stated as a percentage of its par value. For example, a bond with a price of 100 is selling at 100% of its par value, or $1,000 (100% of $1,000). A bond with a price of 90 is selling at a discount equal to 90% of its par value, or $900. A bond with a price of 110 is selling at a premium equivalent to 110% of its par value, or $1,100.

Redeeming Bonds

When a bond reaches its maturity date, the bondholder will redeem it to the issuer and receive the bond's par value plus her last interest payment. At this point, the issuer's obligation to the bondholder has ended and the debt is considered retired. However, some bonds are redeemed before they mature.

Call Provisions

If a bond offering has a call feature attached, the issuer has the ability to redeem the outstanding bonds before the ultimate maturity. If called, the investor receives the full return of principal plus any accrued interest. For the issuer, the benefit is that it's no longer required to make periodic interest payments once the bond issue has been called.

Put Provisions

A bond may also be issued with a put provision, which is the opposite of a call provision. This feature gives the bondholder the right to redeem her bond on a specified date (or dates) prior to maturity. The bondholder usually receives a return of the bond's par value, but the bond may also be redeemable at a discount or premium. A put provision is a benefit to bondholders since it allows investors to redeem the bonds if interest rates rise and to reinvest their funds elsewhere. In an effort to entice investors to buy callable bonds, the yields on callable bonds are higher than those of non-callable bonds. However, for bonds that offer the put feature, their yields are generally lower since the bondholders are given the ability to redeem their bonds in the event that interest rates rise.

Tax Issues with Debt Securities

Two of the primary concerns are 1) how the interest is received and taxed, and 2) how will the gains or losses that are generated by the sale or retirement of the bonds be treated. Capital gains and losses are determined in a manner that's similar to what was addressed in the Equities. In other words, gains and losses are based on the bond's cost basis compared to the proceeds received from the sale. However, when bonds are purchased at prices other than par, the IRS may require that the cost basis be adjusted over the life of the bond.

Taxation of Interest

The interest received from an investment in a corporate bond is taxed at the same rate as the investor's ordinary income. The interest is subject to federal, state, and local taxation and taxable in the year in which it's received. If a corporate bond is sold in the secondary market, the seller must include the amount of accrued interest received and treat it as ordinary income. When reporting income, the buyer must include the amount of the interest payment minus any accrued interest paid at the time of purchase.

Taxation of Zero Coupon

Bonds Under IRS rules, investors who purchase certain low-coupon or zero-coupon bonds are typically required to adjust their cost basis annually. On an annual basis, the discount must be accounted for by using an adjustment method that's referred to as accretion.

Taxation of Premium Bonds

Investors who purchase corporate bonds at a premium must also adjust their cost basis through a process that's referred to as amortization. For example, if a bond is purchased at 110 and it has 10 years to maturity, the bond's cost basis will be adjusted downward by 1-point each year (the 10-point premium is divided by 10 years).

CORPORATE DEBT

Corporations use the funds they raise from issuing bonds for a variety of purposes, from building facilities to purchasing equipment, to expanding their business. The advantage of issuing bonds over stock is that the corporation does not give up partial control of the company or give up a portion of its profits. The downside is that it's required to repay the money borrowed with interest. The requirement to make semiannual interest payments will lower the corporation's profits for as long as it has debt outstanding.

Types of Corporate Bonds

Corporate bonds are divided into two major categories—secured and unsecured. Although all debt that's issued by a corporation is backed by the full faith and credit of the issuer, secured bonds are additionally backed by specific corporate assets.

Secured Bonds

With secured bonds, if the issuer falls into bankruptcy, an appointed trustee will take possession of the assets and liquidate them on the bondholders' behalf. Therefore, secured bondholders have a higher degree of protection if the company defaults. The following are the major types of secured bonds that companies issue: Mortgage Bonds, Equipment Trust Certificates, and Collateral Trust Bonds.

Unsecured Bonds

When corporate bonds are backed by only the corporation's full faith and credit, these forms of unsecured debt are referred to as notes and debentures. If the issuer defaults, the holders of these securities will have the same claim on the company's assets as any other general creditor—which means before the stockholders, but after secured bondholders. Occasionally, companies issue unsecured bonds that have a junior claim on their assets compared to its outstanding unsecured bonds. These bonds are referred to as subordinated debentures. In case of default, the claims of these bondholders are subordinate to those of the other bondholders, but still before the stockholders. Examples are: High-Yield (Junk) Bond, Income Bonds, Guaranteed Bonds, Stepped Coupon Bonds, Zero-Coupon Bonds.

Money-Market Securities

Short-term debt instruments with one year or less to maturity are referred to as money-market securities. There are a significant number of securities that trade in the money market with issuers including the U.S. government, government agencies, banks, and corporations. There is also a diverse group of participants that utilize the money market including the Federal Reserve Board, banks, securities dealers, and corporations. Money-market transactions provide an avenue for both acquiring money (borrowing) and investing (lending) excess funds for short periods. Typically, the investment period ranges from overnight to a few months but maybe as long as one year. Examples of money-market securities and related instruments include Commercial paper, Bankers' acceptances, Negotiable certificates of deposit, Federal funds, Money-market funds, and Repurchase agreements (Repos).

Convertible Bonds

In order to offer investors more of an incentive to buy its bonds, a corporation with a weak credit rating may issue convertible bonds. Similar to convertible preferred stock that was covered earlier, a convertible bond allows an investor to convert the par value of the bond into a predetermined number of shares of the company's common stock. For the purchaser, the tradeoff for this opportunity is that convertible issues traditionally offer lower coupons than similar non-convertible issues. If the bonds are converted, the debt becomes equity and the issuers' capital structure will be significantly altered.

Arbitrage

Arbitrage is a technique that involves profiting from price differentials in the same or similar security. There are times when the market price of a convertible bond does not reflect the value of the common stock that would be received if the bond was converted into stock. If this situation occurs, the convertible bond will be selling at a discount to parity and arbitrageurs could profit from this differential.

Structured products

Structured products are derivative securities that may be linked to a variety of underlying (reference) assets including a stock index, foreign currency, commodity, basket of securities, change in the spread between asset classes, single security, or an interest-rate, and inflation-linked product. A structured product is typically built around a fixed-income instrument (a note) and a derivative product. While the note pays a specified rate of interest to the investor at defined intervals, the derivative component establishes the amount of payment at maturity. These products are considered a form of corporate debt and are typically created by major financial services institutions. Structured products are usually registered as securities with the SEC, clients must receive disclosure that these products are NOT bank deposits and are NOT insured by the Federal Deposit Insurance Corporation (FDIC).

Exchange-Traded Notes (ETNs)

An exchange-traded note (ETN) is a type of unsecured debt security but differs from other types of fixed-income securities since ETN returns are often linked to the performance of an index (some ETN returns may be linked to a commodity or currency). ETNs don't usually pay an annual coupon (they are zero-coupon-like) or specified dividends, instead, all gains are paid at maturity.

Reverse Convertible Securities

Despite their name, these derivative products are NOT like typical corporate bonds; instead, they are a form of a structured product. Reverse convertible securities are short-term notes that are issued by banks and broker-dealers. Although often described as debt instruments, they are far more complex than traditional bonds and involve elements of options trading. Reverse convertibles usually pay a coupon rate that is set above prevailing market rates; however, in return, the buyer may be required to take possession of the shares of an underlying asset. In other words, the issuer agrees to pay a higher coupon in return for the ability to repay the principal to the investor in the form of a set amount of the underlying asset (rather than in cash).

TYPES OF INVESTMENT COMPANIES

An investment company pools funds from numerous investors and purchases securities that are held in a portfolio for the benefit of those investors. The method by which investment companies are organized and operated is governed by the Investment Company Act of 1940.

The Act of 1940 identifies three different types of investment companies—face-amount certificate companies, unit investment trusts, and management companies. The Act further divides the management companies into closed-end and open-end companies. Open-end management companies are more commonly referred to as mutual funds.

Open-End Management Companies (Mutual Funds)

Open-end management companies are by far the most popular type of investment company. The basic idea is that, for a cost, a mutual fund provides a means for investors with similar goals (e.g., long-term growth) to pool their money and invest in a portfolio of securities. As with other companies, this investment pool elects a board of directors (BOD). A mutual fund's BOD will hire an expert (i.e., an investment adviser) to perform the security selection and trading functions.

Other Types of Investment Companies

Face-Amount Certificate Company

This type of investment company is very rare today. A face-amount certificate company issues debt certificates that pay a predetermined rate of interest. Investors purchase these certificates in either periodic installments or by depositing a lump sum and then receive a fixed amount if they hold the certificates until maturity. However, investors who cash in their certificates early will receive a lesser amount—referred to as a surrender value.

Unit Investment Trust

Unit investment trusts (UITs) are formed under a legal document called an indenture and have trustees rather than boards of directors. UITs invest in a fixed portfolio of income-producing securities, such as bonds or preferred stocks. UITs issue only redeemable securities that are referred to as units or shares of beneficial interest (SBIs) that are generally sold in minimum denominations of $1,000. Each unit entitles the holder to an undivided interest in the UIT's portfolio that's proportionate to the amount of money invested. Since the portfolio of a UIT generally remains static until the trust is dissolved, there's no need for an adviser to manage the trust. Since securities are not consistently being purchased or sold, UITs don't have an associated management fee. Without management, there's no management fee that applies. Because of this structure, UITs are considered to be supervised—not managed.

Closed-End Investment Companies

Along with open-ends, closed-end investment companies are the other type of management company. Unlike open-end management companies (mutual funds), closed-end funds usually issue common shares to the public on a one-time basis. Although they may issue additional shares later, they don't continuously issue new shares or stand ready to redeem their shares for cash. While it's typical for closed-end funds to issue common shares, some may issue senior securities (i.e., preferred stock or bonds). Once a closed-end investment company issues shares, these securities trade in the secondary market. Therefore, if an investor wants to purchase shares in a closed-end investment company, he/she will need to buy them on a traditional exchange (e.g., the NYSE or Nasdaq). There's no prospectus delivery requirement that applies to secondary market trades of closed-end funds.

The price that an investor pays for his shares is determined by the market forces of supply and demand. Unlike mutual funds, closed-end funds may trade at prices that are at a discount or a premium to their NAV.

Exchange-Traded Funds (ETFs)

ETFs issue shares each of which represents an interest in an underlying basket of securities that mirror a specific index. Some ETFs may also be linked to indexes that represent the securities of a particular country or industry. Some examples of ETFs include SPDRs (Spiders), which tracks the S&P 500 Index, QQQs (Cubes), which tracks the Nasdaq 100 Index, and DIA (DIAMONDS), which tracks the Dow Jones Industrial Average.

Many investors actively trade ETFs because they think they are better able to estimate the overall direction of the market or a sector, instead of trying to do the same for an individual stock that's more susceptible to unexpected news events. There are a number of ways that ETFs are unlike mutual funds, such as the fact that they are traded on an exchange, have prices that are determined continuously by the forces of supply and demand, have lower expenses, may be sold short, and may be purchased on margin.

An ETF may be an appropriate investment for customers who are investing a lump-sum and are seeking diversification and low costs. They may also be suitable for investors intending to implement asset allocation plans.

ALTERNATIVE INVESTMENTS

Real Estate Investment Trusts (REITs)

Although real estate investment trusts have features that are similar to investment companies, these products are not categorized under the Investment Company Act of 1940. However, the Securities Act of 1933 regulates REITs as securities and requires the sending of prospectuses to any investors who acquire the shares through public offerings conducted in the primary market.

REITs create a portfolio of real estate investments from which investors may earn profits. REITs invest in many different types of residential and commercial income-producing real estate, such as apartment buildings, shopping centers, office complexes, storage facilities, hospitals, and nursing homes. Income is received from the rental income being paid by tenants that leases the real estate which is owned by the REIT. These investments are actually suitable for both retail and institutional investors.

Tax Treatment of REITs

The benefit of qualifying as a real estate investment trust is the favorable tax treatment that's provided under the Internal Revenue Code. Unlike other corporations, there's no double taxation on the dividends that a REIT pays to its shareholders. If 90% of the ordinary income generated from the portfolio is distributed to investors, the income will only be taxed once (at the investors' levels). The REIT avoids paying taxes on distributed income in substantially the same manner as a regulated investment company. However, unlike DPPs, REITs don't pass-through operating losses.

Direct Participation Programs (DPPs)

A direct participation program is a type of investment in which the results of the business venture (cash flow, profits, and losses) directly flow through to the investors. Although DPPs come in different forms, such as general partnerships, joint ventures, and Subchapter S Corporations, the Series 7 Exam tends to focus its questions on limited partnerships. At a minimum, a limited partnership simply requires two partners—one general partner and one limited partner. The general partner (GP) is responsible for managing the program and must contribute at least 1% of the program's capital. The limited partner (LP) is a passive investor who has no control over managerial decisions. Instead, limited partners are typically relied on to contribute a large amount of the program's capital.

Hedge Funds

Hedge funds are private investment pools that are not required to register with the SEC under the Investment Company Act of 1940. These investments are often sold under a Regulation D (private placement) exemption and their purchasers are typically institutional and high net worth investors that can understand the unique risks associated with these products, such as their lack of liquidity and the potential use of leverage by the fund managers. These funds typically have high minimum initial investment requirements (often $1 million or greater).

Business Development Companies (BDCs)

A business development company (BDC) is a type of publicly traded investment company that's designed to aid in the process of capital formation (raising money) for small and middle-market companies. Since BDCs raise money through public offerings, there's no requirement for investors to meet the sophistication, income, or net worth requirements.

OPTIONS

An option is derivative security and, in the simplest terms, is a contract with a value that's derived from the movement of an underlying stock, bond, index, currency, or other assets. These derivatives trade in markets that are very similar to those in which stocks and bonds trade.

The four basic equity option positions are: buying a call, selling a call, buying a put, and selling a put. These four strategies may be used to make simple directional bets on a variety of underlying assets, such as individual security or an index.

The two types of options are calls **and puts.**

1. A call option gives the owner the right to buy the underlying security. In other words, a call buyer is able to call the security away from the writer at a fixed price. The writer of the call has the corresponding obligation to sell the security at the fixed price if the owner exercises the contract.

    Simply stated, the owner of a call has the right to buy stock, while the writer of the call has the obligation to sell a stock.

2. A put option gives the owner the right to sell the underlying security. In other words, a put buyer is able to put the security to the writer at a fixed price. The writer of the put has the corresponding obligation to buy the security at the fixed price if the owner exercises the contract. Ultimately, the owner of a put has the right to sell a stock, while the writer of the put has the obligation to buy stock

Taxation of Options

The tax treatment of an option depends on the manner in which the option is disposed of. The holder (owner) of an option may dispose of the option through any of the following means: 1. Expiration 2. Liquidation 3. Exercise

Expiration of Options

If an option ultimately expires unexercised, the premium will represent either a capital gain or capital loss for tax purposes. For a buyer, the premium paid is a capital loss; however, for a seller, the premium received is a capital gain.

Liquidation of Options

When an investor executes an opposite transaction on the same option, the result is a realized capital gain or a capital loss. Remember, an opening purchase is offset with a closing sale and an opening sale is offset with a closing purchase.

Exercising of Options

Depending on whether an investor is in a position to buy stock or sell stock due to the exercise of an option, the exercise may result in the need to determine the investor's basis or sales proceeds. Since buyers of calls and sellers of puts are in a position to acquire stock as the result of exercise, they are required to calculate the cost basis (the total cost to acquire). On the other hand, since buyers of puts and sellers of calls are in a position to deliver stock as the result of exercise, they are required to calculate sales proceeds (the total money received on delivery).

CHAPTER 10
REAL ESTATE LAW

I'm dedicating this chapter to certain topics about Real Estate Florida Law simply to make you aware of some of the terminologies.

Definition: Real Property

Real property or real estate means any interest or estate in land and any interest in business enterprises or business opportunities, including any assignment, leasehold, sub leasehold, or mineral right. However, the term does not include any cemetery lot or right of burial in any cemetery, nor does the term include the renting of a mobile home lot or recreational vehicle lot in a mobile home park or travel park.

Real Property vs. Personal Property

Real property is basically land and improvements to the land. Property that is not real property is personal property (also called chattel). Personal property usually consists of items having a limited life that are easily movable from one place to another. Just as the term realty is used to denote real property, the term personalty is used to indicate personal property. It is important to distinguish between real property and personal property in a real estate transaction. All personal property included in the sale should be identified in the contract for sale, or the seller is entitled to remove the property.

Estates and Tenancies

An estate refers to the degree, quantity, nature, and extent of interest a person can have in real property. The terms estate and tenancy are to be used interchangeably. Estates are divided into the following two general groups, (1) Freehold estates, which are for an indefinite length (of unknown duration), and (2) Leasehold estates, which are for a fixed term (known duration).

Sole Ownership vs. Concurrent Ownership

When title to the property is held by one person, it creates an estate in severalty or sole ownership. Separate property is a property that a spouse owns in the spouse's name only before marriage and property acquired by one spouse during the marriage by inheritance or gift.

Property acquired during the marriage, except by inheritance or gift, is referred to as marital assets. For example, one spouse may purchase a property with her own savings and title the property in her name only. Unless the couple signed a prenuptial agreement, the property is legally a marital asset. If the couple later divorces the courts will divide marital property "equitably."

Ownership of property by two or more persons at the same time is concurrent ownership. There are three types of estates (tenancies) with concurrent owners: tenancy in common, joint tenancy, and tenancy by the entireties.

THREE TYPES OF ESTATES

Tenancy in Common

When two or more persons wish to share the ownership of a single property, they may choose to do so as tenants in common. It is the most frequently used form of co-ownership, except for husband-and-wife ownership. Tenants in common may acquire title on the same or different deeds, at the same or different times, and with equal or unequal shares of ownership. As tenants in common, each owns an "undivided interest" in the whole property. An undivided interest is an interest in the entire property, rather than ownership of a particular part of the property.

Joint Tenancy

A major difference between a joint tenancy and a tenancy in common is that joint tenancy is characterized by the right of survivorship. Right of survivorship means that the share of a co-owner who has died goes to the surviving co-owner(s) and not to the deceased tenant's heirs. Joint tenants have an undivided interest in real property.

Tenancy by the Entireties

A tenancy by the entireties is basically a joint tenancy between a married couple. Any type of property (residential, commercial, industrial, and so forth) purchased by a married couple together, will be held as a tenancy by the entireties. The deed or other instrument of conveyance does not have to state expressly that a tenancy by the entireties exists. If the parties are truly married to each other, the estate is implied. While not mandatory, the deed should reflect a tenancy by the entireties to serve notice to others that such an estate exists, such as John P. Smith and Sally R. Smith, a married couple.

One spouse cannot do anything that affects the ownership of a tenancy by the entireties, such as a mortgage, will, or sell any portion of the spousal interest in a tenancy by the entireties without the other spouse's consent. When one spouse dies, that individual's ownership interest automatically transfers to the surviving spouse by the right of survivorship. The surviving spouse will then own the property in fee simple. If the married couple divorces, all property owned as a tenancy by the entireties will automatically become a tenancy in common, with each former spouse having an equal share in the property.

Cooperatives

A cooperative, cooperative association or co-op is a multi-unit building that is owned by a corporation. The corporation holds title to the land and improvements. The unit owners purchase shares of stock in the corporation. Ownership of the stock entitles the purchaser to a proprietary lease and the right to occupy the unit.

Condominiums

A condominium consists of condominium units and common elements. Condominiums may look like apartment buildings, attached townhouses, or freestanding houses; what makes the structures condominiums is how the developer organized the association. The Condominium Act provides that an association, usually a not-for-profit corporation, is responsible for operating the condominium. The condominium association is run by a board of directors, initially appointed by the developer, and subsequently turned over to elected directors.

A condo purchaser owns an individual unit in fee simple. The deed to the unit may be held by one or more persons in any type of estate or tenancy recognized by state law. The unit owner also owns an undivided fractional (proportionate) share of the common elements. Common elements are those portions of the condominium property that are not included in the units but are legally attached to each unit and are transferred with the unit when it is sold. A deed to a unit conveys the unit to the purchaser together with its proportionate ownership interest in the common elements. Property taxes are levied on individual units.

Time-Sharing

Time-sharing evolved out of the vacation condominium concept. The property is first organized as a condominium. Each unit is divided into time intervals of ownership, usually 52 weeks. A deed or some evidence of share ownership or right of occupancy is prepared for each time interval. Time-share ownership involves an undivided interest in a living unit according to the number of weeks purchased. For example, if one week is purchased, the buyer owns a 1/52 interest in the unit. Size, location, amenities, and time of year all affect the purchase price of the time-share unit.

Legal vs. Equitable Title to Real Property

A person who holds ownership rights in property is said to have a title to the property. **Legal title** is ownership of a freehold estate. Freehold estates include fee simple estates and life estates. Title to real property is a legal concept signifying ownership of the collection of rights called an *estate*.

The equitable title implies that an individual will receive a legal title at a future date. When the buyer and seller execute the sale contract the buyer receives equitable title to the property. The law recognizes some ownership interest by the buyer even though the buyer is not yet the owner of the record.

Protection of Title

A chain of title is the complete successive record of a property's ownership. Beginning with the earliest owner, the title may pass to many individuals. Each owner is "linked" to the next so that a "chain" is formed. A chain of title can be traced through linking conveyances from the present owner back to the earliest recorded owner.

Abstract of Title

An abstract of title is a search of the recorded documents concerning a parcel of real property. It is a condensed history that discloses those items about the property that are of public record. An abstract is conducted to determine the legal owner of the property and to reveal any mortgages, liens, judgments, or unpaid taxes that have not been satisfied to date. All recorded liens and encumbrances are included, along with their current status. The abstract of title does not guarantee or ensure the validity of the title of the property. The abstract of title does not reveal such items as encroachments or forgeries, or any interests or conveyances that have not been recorded.

Title Opinion

Some buyers will accept an opinion of title executed by an attorney who has studied the abstract of title.

The opinion will list any defects or clouds on the title, such as liens, easements, or other encumbrances, and it will include the attorney's opinion of whether the seller has a *marketable title*. Most attorneys do not guarantee the opinion of title. It is an opinion only, backed by legal training and experience. If the opinion should prove to be in error, negligence must usually be proved for the attorney's client to receive reimbursement.

Title Insurance

The limited protection afforded buyers of real property by an opinion of title led to the need for title insurance. Title insurance is a contract that protects the policyholder from losses arising from defects in the title.

Deeds

A deed is a written instrument that conveys title to real property. It is an instrument of conveyance whereby title to real property is transferred from one party to another. The two parties to a deed are the grantor (owner giving title) and the grantee (new owner receiving title). Title passes at the time of voluntary delivery and acceptance when the grantor delivers a valid deed that is accepted by the grantee.

TYPES OF STATUTORY DEEDS

A statutory deed is a deed whose format is defined by state law. Florida law provides for a short form of deed in which the covenants or warranties mentioned are implied to exist just as though they were written out in complete and detailed form. There are four types of statutory deeds: (1) quitclaim deed, (2) bargain and sale deed, (3) special warranty deed, and (4) general warranty deed.

Quitclaim Deed

A quitclaim deed provides the least protection to the grantee. A quitclaim deed contains a premises section with a granting clause that conveys what interest (if any) the grantor may have when the deed is delivered. The grantor makes no warranties about the quality or extent of the title being conveyed. Quitclaim deeds are used to clear existing or potential clouds on the title. To clear the title of possible trouble spots and defects, the grantor releases any claim or interest in the property. Words of conveyance used in a quitclaim deed are remise, release, and quitclaim.

Bargain and Sale Deed

A bargain and sale deed is similar to a quitclaim deed because the grantor makes no warranties about the quality or extent of the title being conveyed. Unlike the quitclaim deed, the bargain and sale deed contains a seisin clause indicating the grantor has title to the property. However, the grantor makes no express warranty against encumbrances.

Special Warranty Deed

A **special warranty deed** is similar to the bargain and sale deed because it contains a seisin clause indicating the grantor has title to the property. Like the bargain and sale deed, the special warranty deed uses the words grants, bargains, and sales. An important distinction between a bargain and sale deed and a special warranty deed is that the grantor in a special warranty deed guarantees the title against title defects arising during the period of the grantor's ownership of the property, but not against defects existing before that time.

General Warranty Deed

The general warranty deed provides the greatest protection to the buyer because the general warranty deed contains all the covenants and warranties available to give the grantee every possible future guarantee to title protection.

GOVERNMENT RESTRICTIONS ON OWNERSHIP

The three most important subcategories of governmental limitations on ownership of real property are (1) police power, (2) eminent domain, and (3) taxation.

Police Power

The U.S. and state constitutions provide for the government to apply restrictions deemed necessary in the interest of the general health, welfare, or safety of its citizens. Under police power, the use of real property may be regulated. From these powers come the many ordinances and regulations governing zoning, building codes, health standards, city planning, and rent controls. Police power represents the broadest power of the government to limit or regulate the rights of property owners.

Eminent Domain

Eminent domain is called taking for just compensation. The constitutions of the U.S. government and state governments grant the power (right) to take private property for public use. The U.S. Constitution prohibits taking private property for a public purpose without just compensation. Condemnation is the process by which the government exercises eminent domain, by either judicial or administrative proceedings.

Property Taxation

This power was specifically limited to the various states by the U.S. Constitution. Citizens pay for the benefits and protection provided by the various levels of government. Property is usually the primary basis for local taxation. Local taxing authorities can foreclose on real property for nonpayment of taxes.

LIENS

A lien is a claim to have a debt or other obligation satisfied out of property belonging to another. Common examples are mortgage liens, construction liens, property tax liens, and judgment liens. Liens can entitle the holder (lienor) to have the property sold, regardless of the desires of the owner (lienee).

Liens are usually recorded with the clerk of the circuit court in the county where the property is located. A lien is an encumbrance on the title to real property. However, not all encumbrances on the property are liens. Encumbrances can also be easements, covenants, deed restrictions, encroachments, and governmental regulations.

LIEN PRIORITY

When there are two or more liens on a property, the *priority* of the liens determines the order in which the liens will be satisfied (paid off) if the property must be sold. Lien priority is important because the lienor (the creditor) receives no compensation until all liens senior to the lienor's lien have been fully satisfied. Once a lien has been satisfied, a *release* or *satisfaction* of the lien should be recorded to remove the lien.

Superior Liens

Superior liens take priority over all other liens. They are automatically *superior* to any other lien. Three superior liens are Real estate (property) tax liens, Special assessment liens, and Federal estate tax lien (at time of death).

Junior Liens

The priority of junior liens is based on the date of recording in the public records. The priority of most liens is the date and time that the lien was recorded in the public records. Four important junior liens are Mortgage liens, Judgment liens, Vendor's liens, and Income tax (IRS) liens.

Construction Liens

Construction liens (also called mechanics' liens) are an exception to the priority rule regarding the recording date. A construction lien's priority in a foreclosure sale is retroactive to the date the work was first performed or materials were first delivered to the property.

Subordination Agreement

The priority of liens may be changed by a written agreement called a subordination agreement. Under a subordination agreement, the holder of a prior lien (lien with an earlier recording date) agrees to allow a junior lienholder's interest to move ahead of the prior lien.

CONTRACTS IN GENERAL

A contract defines the parties' legal relationship and spells out each party's rights and duties. It is a voluntary agreement or promise between legally competent parties, supported by legal consideration, to perform (or refrain from performing) some legal act.

Underlying every contract is the promise. In a real estate contract, the seller promises to convey title to the real estate, and the buyer promises to pay the purchase price. Contract promises are enforceable by law, provided the contract meets certain requirements.

Statute of Frauds

The statute of frauds requires that contracts conveying an interest in real property and all contracts that are not performed within one year from the date they become effective must be in writing and signed to be enforceable. An enforceable contract is a contract that the courts will recognize as legally binding.

Statute of Limitations

The statute of limitations is the period of time, set by statute, during which the terms of a contract may be enforced. It protects people from being compelled to perform or otherwise be sued after a period of time has expired. The times vary, depending on whether it is an oral contract or a written contract: (1) Written contracts—five years, (2) Oral contracts—four years, (3) Partly written and partly oral, five years for the written portion and four years for the oral portion.

TRANSFER OF REAL PROPERTY

Like all contracts, real estate purchase contracts must contain the four essential elements to be valid. Furthermore, to be enforceable in court, real estate purchase contracts must be in writing and signed by all parties who are bound by the agreement. Real estate purchase contracts are not required to be witnessed or notarized. Real estate contracts are not recorded.

A void contract lacks one or more of the required elements of a valid contract and, therefore, has no legal effect. A contract that is void was never a legal contract. For example, the use of a forged name in a listing contract would make the contract void.

A voidable contract allows one of the parties to potentially disavow contractual duties.

An unenforceable contract will not be enforced by a court of law. For example, a contract may be unenforceable because the statute of limitations has passed. Void contracts are also unenforceable contracts. An oral contract for sale and purchase of real estate may otherwise be valid but unenforceable because the statute of frauds requires such contracts to be in writing.

MORTGAGE LAW

Lien Theory

Today, most states, including Florida, are lien theory states.
The *borrower* retains title to the property. The lender is protected with a lien on the real property to secure the payment of the mortgage debt. If the borrower defaults on the mortgage debt, the lender will foreclose to recover the money owed.

Title Theory

In some states, title to the mortgaged property is conveyed to the *lender* through a mortgage deed or to a trustee through a deed of trust. This mortgage theory is called title theory. If the borrower defaults, the lender may take possession of the property. The borrower retains equitable title to the property. Once the debt is paid in full, the lender conveys legal title to the borrower.

Two instruments are involved in a mortgage loan: (1) the *promissory note*, which is the actual promise to repay, and (2) the *mortgage,* which creates the lien interest.

MORTGAGE PROVISION

A prepayment clause allows the borrower to pay off part or all of the debt, without penalty or other fees, before maturity. A prepayment clause is normally included in FHA and VA mortgages on real property. A prepayment clause typically stipulates conditions and terms under which the mortgage loan may be prepaid.

Prepayment Penalty Clause

The lender may choose to charge a prepayment penalty for early payment if provided for in the mortgage instrument.

Acceleration Clause

The acceleration clause authorizes the mortgagee to accelerate or advance the due date of the entire unpaid balance if the mortgagor fails to fulfill any promises stated in the mortgage instrument.

The acceleration clause gives the lender the power to declare the entire unpaid mortgage loan due and payable and to foreclose on the property if the mortgagor does not remedy the default.

Right to Reinstate

This clause provides for the mortgagor's right to reinstate the original repayment terms in the note after the mortgagee has initiated the acceleration clause. It gives the mortgagor the right to have foreclosure proceedings stopped before the foreclosure sale, provided the mortgagor pays all sums that would be due if no acceleration had occurred plus all expenses incurred by the mortgagee in enforcing the mortgage.

Due-on-Sale Clause

The due-on-sale clause allows the mortgagee (lender) to demand the outstanding loan balance plus accrued interest. If the property or any interest in the property is sold or transferred without the lender's prior written consent, the lender may require immediate payment in full.

Defeasance Clause

The defeasance clause is so named because it "defeats" the prior action when the borrower-mortgagor has made the final payment on the loan. Recall that in title theory states, the mortgaged property is conveyed to the lender through a mortgage deed. Therefore, title theory states, the defeasance clause defeats the conveyance of legal title and returns the legal title to the borrower-mortgagor. In lien theory states, the lender is protected with a lien on the property that pledges the property as collateral until the debt is paid in full. Once the debt is repaid, the defeasance clause defeats the mortgage lien and the property is no longer pledged as collateral.

MORTGAGE FEATURES

Down Payment

The down payment is the amount of cash a purchaser will pay at the time of purchase. Any earnest money pledged when the original offer to purchase was made is applied toward the total amount of cash down payment due at closing.

Loan-to-Value Ratio (LTV)

The loan-to-value ratio (LTV) is the relationship between the amount borrowed and the appraised value (or purchase price) of a property. Lenders use this ratio as the measure of financial risk associated with lending and borrowing money. The higher the LTV (or the greater the loan compared with the property's value), the lower the lender's safety cushion should the borrower default.

Equity

An owner's equity in the property is the monetary interest the owner has in property over and above the mortgage indebtedness. When purchasing a property, the owner's initial equity is the down payment. The greater an owner's equity, the less risk for the mortgagee.

Interest

Interest is the cost for the use of borrowed funds. A lender charges interest on the remaining principal balance (the amount borrowed) over the life of the loan. Interest may be due at either the end of the payment period or at the beginning of each payment period. Payments made at the end of a payment period are called payments in arrears. This payment method is the general practice, and mortgages often call for end-of-period payments due on the first of the following month. Payments may also be made at the beginning of each period and are called payments in advance.

Loan Servicing

Some lenders handle the loan payment collection and recordkeeping for the mortgages they originate. Loan servicing is an additional source of income for lenders. Servicing fees typically range from ⅜ to ¾ of 1% of the unpaid balance of loans serviced. Lenders are generally willing to retain servicing of any loans sold to institutional investors.

Escrow (Impound) Account

Most lenders require borrowers to pay, in advance, monthly installments for property taxes and hazard insurance. The monthly escrow payment is one-twelfth of the estimated annual expense for property taxes and the hazard insurance premium. These payments are held in an escrow (impound) account for the borrower. When the taxes and insurance premiums become due, the lender pays the expenses out of the escrow account.

Federal regulations limit the total amount of reserves that lenders may require. Holding funds in an escrow account to cover ongoing expenses associated with the property protects lenders from defaults, tax liens, and catastrophe.

PITI

The monthly mortgage payment paid by the borrower consists of principal and interest on the loan and the monthly reserve for property taxes and hazard insurance. The monthly principal, interest, taxes, and insurance payment is called PITI.

Discount Points

Discount points are an added loan fee often charged by lenders to increase the yield on a lower-than-market-interest loan and to make the loan more competitive with higher-interest loans. Borrowers often pay discount points upfront in order to gain a long-term, lower interest rate. The lower interest rate loan is advantageous to a homebuyer who plans to keep the loan for several years. This extra up-front fee is a prepaid interest that increases the real yield, or annual percentage rate (APR), to the lender, making discount points advantageous for the lender.

Loan Origination Fee

The processing of a mortgage application is called loan origination. Lenders typically charge the borrower a loan origination fee. Amounts vary, but the fee is typically 1% or 2% of the loan amount. The lender also charges the borrower all expenses encountered in obtaining credit reports, preparing loan documents, and processing a mortgage loan application.

Assignment of Mortgage

When a homebuyer borrows money to purchase a home, the borrower (mortgagor) signs a promissory note and mortgage instrument. The mortgage and promissory note are the property of the mortgagee (lender). The mortgagee may choose to sell the negotiable instruments rather than continue to receive the monthly payments from the mortgagor.

When ownership of a mortgage is transferred from one company or individual to another, it is called an assignment. This process is accomplished by executing an assignment of mortgage. The assignment of mortgage is a legal instrument stating that the mortgagee assigns (transfers) the mortgage and promissory note to the purchaser. The assignment of mortgage is signed by the assignor (mortgagee) and delivered to the assignee (investor). The assignee becomes the new owner of the debt and security instrument.

The individual or company purchasing the mortgage will receive an estoppel certificate (estoppel letter) verifying the amount of the unpaid balance, the rate of interest, and the date to which interest has been paid before the assignment. The purpose of an estoppel certificate is to stop a claim that the amount owed is different from the actual unpaid balance or that the interest rate is an amount other than the contracted rate. If requested, the mortgagee must provide an estoppel letter to the mortgagor.

Contract for Deed (Land Contract)

A contract for deed is used to finance the sale of the property when a buyer does not have sufficient cash to make a down payment large enough to secure traditional financing. The buyer agrees to the purchase price for the property, typically makes a small down payment, and pays monthly payments of principal and interest to the seller. The buyer takes possession of the property at closing; however, instead of receiving a deed, the purchaser receives a contract for deed, giving the buyer equitable title to the property. Equitable title entitles the buyer to homestead protection. The buyer is responsible for the expenses associated with ownership, including the real estate property taxes, property insurance, and upkeep. The seller retains legal title to the property until the debt is repaid. Once repaid, the seller delivers a deed and the legal title is conveyed to the buyer

DEFAULT

Foreclosure

The borrower is required to fulfill certain obligations agreed to in the promissory note. These obligations include repayment of the debt, payment of property taxes, maintenance, and upkeep, and keeping the property insured. Failure to meet any of these obligations can result in a borrower's default. When default occurs, the lender has the right under the mortgage contract to pursue legal action against the borrower for payment of the debt. In Florida, foreclosure is a judicial process that requires the mortgagee to file a foreclosure suit in court. Foreclosure is the enforcement of the mortgage lien.

Equity of Redemption

Equity of redemption allows the mortgagor to prevent foreclosure from occurring by paying the mortgagee the principal and interest due plus any expenses the mortgagee has incurred in attempting to collect the debt and initiating foreclosure proceedings. In Florida, the right of equity of redemption ends once the property has been sold at the foreclosure sale.

Results of Foreclosure

If redemption is not made, on confirmation of the sale, the clerk files a certificate of title and title passes to the purchaser. There are no warranties; title passes "as is," although free of the former defaulted mortgage. The successful bidder obtains no better title than the mortgagor held. The doctrine of caveat emptor applies in foreclosure sales; that is, the purchaser is presumed to know that the purchase is subject to any prior liens of record or interests for which there is constructive notice.

Short Sale

A short sale involves a real estate transaction where the net proceeds at closing will not satisfy the payoff amount of mortgages and other liens on the property. The deficiency in funds is because the seller is attempting to sell the home to the buyer for an amount less than the amount owed to the lender(s) and other lienholders (if any).

Sometimes, because of depressed market conditions, a mortgagee will allow a property secured by a mortgage loan to be sold for less money than what is owed to the lender. The lender releases its mortgage so that the property can be sold free and clear to the new purchaser. The lender decides to cut its losses by agreeing to a negotiated sale rather than the delay and expense of a foreclosure action.

Deed in Lieu of Foreclosure

Sometimes the parties will agree to settle the default without going to court. This can be accomplished with a deed in lieu of foreclosure. The process is sometimes called a friendly foreclosure because it is a nonjudicial procedure (it does not involve a lawsuit). The defaulting borrower gives the title (the deed) to the lender to avoid judicial foreclosure. The lender takes title to the property subject to existing liens.

TYPES OF MORTGAGES

Conventional loans

Conventional loans are written by private lenders and are not guaranteed or insured by the federal government. Conventional loans typically require a larger down payment, compared with FHA and VA loans, and therefore have a lower LTV. Borrowers must pay for private mortgage insurance (PMI) for the portion of the loan above 80% LTV. Fixed-rate conventional mortgage loans have a due-on-sale clause, so they are not assumable.

The Federal Housing Administration (FHA)

The Federal Housing Administration (FHA) is a government agency that insures mortgage loans made by approved lenders. FHA does not make loans nor does it regulate interest rates. Borrowers pay an up-front mortgage insurance premium (UFMIP) and an annual mortgage insurance premium (MIP). The annual premium is paid monthly as part of the monthly mortgage payment. Borrowers are required to make a down payment of at least 3.5%. The Section 203(b) FHA program insures fixed-rate loans on one- to four-family residences.

The Department of Veterans Affairs (VA)

The Department of Veterans Affairs (VA) partially guarantees mortgage loans. Private lenders provide VA loans to veterans, surviving spouses of veterans, and active military personnel. The VA also has the power to make direct loans to veterans. A veteran's entitlement is the maximum amount the government guarantees the lender will be paid in the event the borrower defaults. A veteran's certificate of eligibility states the amount of entitlement available to the veteran borrower. Down payments are not required on VA loans that do not exceed $484,350. The VA charges a funding (user) fee to help the government defray the cost of foreclosures. VA loans do not have due-on-sale clauses; therefore, they are assumable (even by nonveterans).

Economic Tools

The Fed has three economic tools to influence money supply: (1) the purchase and sale of U.S. Treasury securities called open-market operations, (2) increasing or decreasing the discount rate charged to banks that borrow money from the Fed, and (3) increasing or decreasing the amount of funds that institutions must hold in reserve against deposit liabilities called the reserve requirement.

Secondary Mortgage Market

A secondary mortgage market is an investor market that buys and sells existing mortgages. Secondary market participants include Fannie Mae, Freddie Mac, and Ginnie Mae. Fannie Mae deals in conventional, FHA, and VA loans. Conforming loans are loans that meet Fannie Mae guidelines. Fannie Mae provides a secondary market for loans originated by commercial banks. Freddie Mac is primarily a secondary market for conventional loans. It provides a secondary market for loans originated by savings associations. Ginnie Mae is a government agency under HUD. Ginnie Mae–approved mortgage-backed securities (MBSs) are the only ones that carry the full faith and credit guarantee of the federal government. The mortgages in these MBSs are mainly FHA and VA mortgages.

The Truth in Lending Act

The Truth in Lending Act is implemented by the Federal Reserve's Regulation Z and requires lenders to disclose the annual percentage rate (APR) and all costs associated with credit. The law gives borrowers three business days to cancel most consumer loan contracts, except loans to purchase or construct a home.

Economic characteristics of real estate

Economic characteristics of real estate include (1) government controls influencing the market through zoning, building codes, and taxes; (2) the market's slow response to changes in supply and demand; (3) area preference (situs) influencing the price buyers are willing to pay; and (4) supply and demand interacting to affect property prices.

APPROACHES TO ESTIMATING VALUE

The three approaches to estimating value are (1) sales comparison approach, (2) cost-depreciation approach, and (3) income approach. The principle of substitution is the basis for all three approaches.

The **sales comparison approach** compares similar properties to the subject property. The comparable properties' sale prices are adjusted upward or downward to reflect differences between each comparable and the subject property. If a comparable is superior to the subject property on a given feature, a downward adjustment is made to the comp. If a comparable is inferior to the subject property, an upward adjustment is made to the comp. The adjusted sale prices of the comparables are reconciled using a weighted average to estimate the market value of the subject property.

The **cost approach** estimates the market value of a property based on the cost to buy an equivalent site and to reproduce the structure as if new, less depreciation. Reproduction cost is the amount of money required to build an exact duplicate of the structure. Replacement cost is the amount of money required to replace a structure having the same use and functional utility as the subject property but using modern, available, or updated materials.

The **income approach** develops an estimated value based on the present worth of future income from the subject property. The approach capitalizes net operating income into value.

CHAPTER 11
THE REWARD

I hope you didn't look at the Table of Contents and go straight to this chapter because you saw the word "reward". Unfortunately, there is no short cut. You must do the work. It took me years to learn what I learned, but be grateful and thank the Universe because it led me to this path. I shared what I learned to help you to the right path quicker. What you read here is valuable information, so congratulation if you are the one who did not skip the 10 chapters. Proud of you!

Regarding the REWARD. You probably think I'm crazy for doing this, but I am not new to the reward system as I explained in the beginning. I like rewards. This is the world I lived in and I am grateful. I give credit to my parents for using positive reinforcement and keeping me motivated growing up and rewarding me with money or things I love to maintain good grades. Okay, you can call it a bribe, but it worked. I was at the top of my graduating class in high school and college. I've used the same strategy with my son and it worked.

For the last 11 years, I served as a Board Member of the Asian American Heritage Council of Central Florida and helped raise funds to be used as Scholarship Awards every year. Due to the pandemic, we were not able to raise funds this year because we did not have our annual cultural festival which is the main source of funds. Please feel free to support our organization if you so desire. We are a 501(c)(3) organization, therefore your generous donation will be a tax write-off, and thank you in advance for supporting our efforts. This is our website: *www.aahc-cf.org.*

I told you I like REWARDS. Now, here are the contest rules.

CONTEST RULES

We will be raffling a 3-night stay at a 5-star Luxury resort every November beginning 2021. Let's make this fun, here are the requirements to participate:

1. After reading this book, provide a review on Amazon.
2. Contact us via our website to inform us of your intent to participate in the raffle and to also let us know your 6-month financial goal. Raffle entry will be open until February. Entries received after February will be entered into the raffle the following year.

3. On or before the end of August, write to us again and update us on your progress, whether or not you achieved your 6- month goal. This must be received no later than August 31st.
4. Whoever participated in 1, 2, and 3 above, will be included in the raffle drawing the first week of September. We will be picking the lucky person via Facebook live. Make sure you join our Facebook group (The Finance Doctor's Tips & Tricks) to stay informed.

This will be an honor system so we will not check whether or not you accomplished what you said you've done, but if you understand the 12 Laws of the Universe, you know better not to cheat.

Oh, you might be wondering why not a monetary reward as the prize instead of the 3-night stay. Two reasons:

1. Money cannot buy "experience."
   Did you not know that 3 things can shape your life? The books you read, the people you meet, and the places you visit. I'm trying to help you accomplish all of that in one seminar.
2. The 3-night stay will be at our annual conference because I want you to share your story with others so you can inspire and motivate them and for you to expand your network and meet like-minded individuals.

If you so desire to be part of our annual conference, inform us right away as it will be a first come first serve basis as the space is very limited. Depending on the demand, semi-annual conferences will be considered.

DAILY CHECKLIST

Before I completely let you go, I put together this checklist that will help you stay on track with your desired goals, whether it be with your relationship, health, or finances. Always remember that everything starts with the mind, when you change your life in the "mental/psychological realm", it's just a matter of time when that gets manifested in the "physical reality". Believe this because it is the law, and this will help you on your journey. It prevents you from being doubtful, fearful, and worrisome. Let me tell you a quick true story. There was a case of a man who feared getting a rare disease. He was so fearful of getting it, he constantly thought about what would happen if he got it. Sure enough, he ended up getting this rare disease.

Remember this story when you catch yourself thinking about negative thoughts. Once you get good at catching yourself thinking negatively, then it's just a matter of time when you can quickly switch your mind to positive thinking. When you consistently practice positivity in your life, in time, your mind becomes purer and purer, your health will improve, your relationships will improve, and your finances will improve. Here is the 10 Daily checklist that will help you stay on track:

1. Am I conforming with the Laws of the Universe, or am I going against the flow that might be causing my misery?
2. Where am I in the Emotion Frequencies scale? Am I vibrating in 500hz and above?
3. Did I use the "Visualize and Feel" manifestation strategy today?
4. How did I add value to others today? Can I do more? (Remember that you must DEPOSIT before you can WITHDRAW)
5. Did I behave or think negatively today? If so, how can I change that and make sure it doesn't happen again?
6. Can the Universe recognize themselves in me, or was I so negative that I pushed them away today?
7. Did I spend time connecting with the Universe through meditation? Am I acting on the message that they are giving me?
8. Am I using both my emotional intelligence and intellect in making important decisions today?
9. Are my actions today helping me become the Master of My Mind and My Life?
10. Did I write at least 3 things I am grateful for today in my gratitude journal?

PARTING WORDS

I hope that this book motivates and inspires you to change your current situation to the life that you dream and wish for. You are so powerful that you can choose to change or not change.

Don't allow limiting beliefs, poverty mindset, negative programming to get in the way of the kind of life you desire. You create your own reality. Your current situation is the result of your past thoughts and actions. It wasn't your spouse, it wasn't your parents, it wasn't your boss.

It was you. It's your reality.

Always have an "End-Result" in mind. "VISUALIZE and FEEL" what it would be like when your wishes and dreams are fulfilled. Doing so will align yourself with the Universe. You have to prove to the Universe that you are worthy of the abundance by doing what it wants you to do i.e. by not going against the Laws of the Universe, by serving others, by following your heart, and by staying in touch with your intuition.

We are one. If you think negatively about others, you just hurt yourself. That negative thought or action will come back to you ten-fold. Always observe and be mindful of your words and actions towards others. Focus on how you can add value to others using your unique gifts and talents. After you proved yourself to the Universe, then abundance will flow. You are not there yet because you have not done the work.

Unfortunately, there is no short cut. I accomplished what I did because of my beliefs, my mindset, my perseverance, my determination, and my faith and trust in God / Divine / Universe - that I can do whatever I set my mind to. When you were binging on Netflix, having drinks with your friends, hanging out at the beach, and on social media, I was continuously learning and improving myself. This is what you need to do until such time that you achieve your goal.

What I shared here is from my experiences, what the Universe channeled to me, the knowledge from books I read, and many courses I took. It's possible that you may have to keep reading this a few more times until you get it, and that's okay. Always be kind to yourself and I suggest you set an intention next time for you to receive what the Universe wants you to get out of this book, so that you may act on that message.

Contact us (https://excelsureconsultingllc.com/contact) if you are participating in our contest, or you want to apply for one-on-one mentorship.

Join us in our **Facebook group: The Finance Doctor's Successful and Happy Beings group** to surround and associate yourself with like-minded people.

I look forward to hearing about your journey and how this book helped you and the people around you. See you at our future conference. Photos attached.

THINK BIG! DREAM BIG!

Declare your SUCCESS today.
"Visualize and Feel" the emotion of joy, satisfaction, and excitement when
you share your SUCCESS story when you join us at our annual conference at some of the Top LUXURIOUS resorts in the world!!!

CLAIM YOUR SUCCESS NOW!

Shangri-La Boracay (Philippines)
(Photo Credit: Resort website)

12 Apostles Hotel (South Africa)

(Photo Credit: Resort website)

Kuda Huraa (Maldives)

(Photo Credit: Resort website)

Six Senses Zil Pasyon (Seychelles)

(Photo Credit: Resort website)

The Wickaninnish Inn (Canada)

(Photo Credit: Resort website)

Amanyara (Turks & Caicos)

(Photo Credit: Resort website)

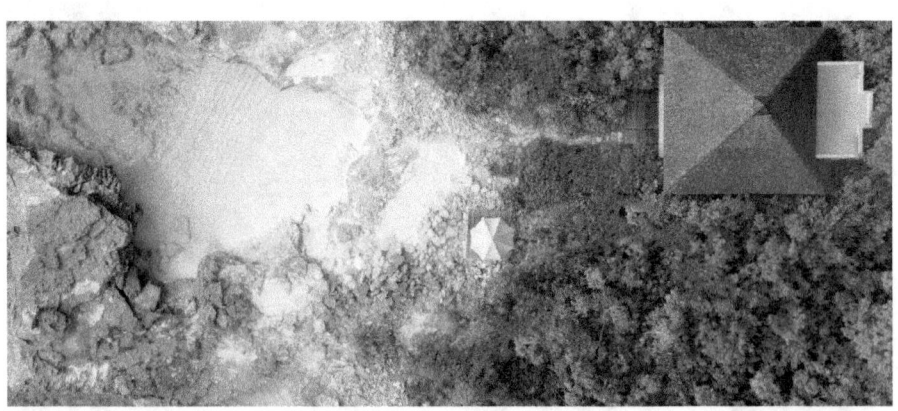

Soneva Kiri (Thailand)

(Photo Credit: Resort website)

St. Regis Bora Bora (French Polynesia)

(Photo Credit: Resort website)

Four Seasons Hualalai (Hawaii)

(Photo Credit: Resort website)

Qualia Great Barrier Reef (Australia)

(Photo Credit: Resort website)

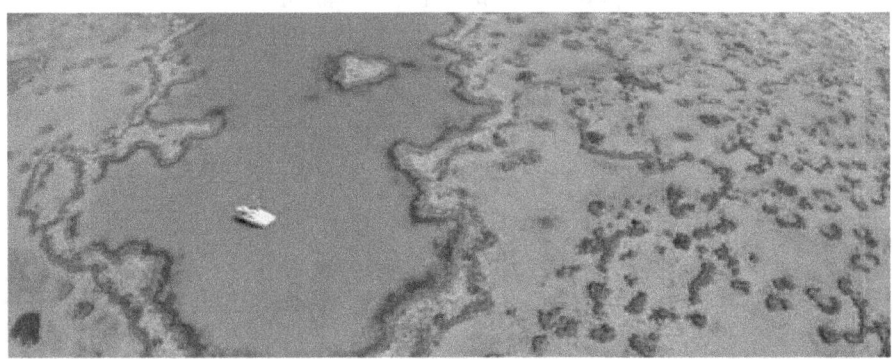

Soneva Jani (Maldives)

(Photo Credit: Resort website)

Amanpulo (Philippines)

(Photo Credit: Resort website)

May YOU be happy.

May YOU be peaceful.

May YOU be liberated from your miseries.

APPENDIX

Income Statement

Name
Time Period

Financial Statements in U.S. Dollars

Revenue
- Gross Sales
- Less: Sales Returns and Allowances
- **Net Sales**

Cost of Goods Sold
- Beginning Inventory
- Add: Purchases
  - Freight-in
  - Direct Labor
  - Indirect Expenses
- Inventory Available
- Less: Ending Inventory
- **Cost of Goods Sold**

Gross Profit (Loss)

Expenses
- Advertising
- Amortization
- Bad Debts
- Bank Charges
- Charitable Contributions
- Commissions
- Contract Labor
- Depreciation
- Dues and Subscriptions
- Employee Benefit Programs
- Insurance
- Interest
- Legal and Professional Fees
- Licenses and Fees
- Miscellaneous
- Office Expense
- Payroll Taxes
- Postage
- Rent
- Repairs and Maintenance
- Supplies
- Telephone
- Travel
- Utilities
- Vehicle Expenses
- Wages
- **Total Expenses**

Net Operating Income

Other Income
- Gain (Loss) on Sale of Assets
- Interest Income
- **Total Other Income**

Net Income (Loss)

NET WORTH BALANCE SHEET

ASSETS:
CASH
- **1.** Cash on Hand $ _____
- **2.** Checking Account $ _____
- **3.** Savings Account $ _____
- **4.** Money Market Funds $ _____
- **5.** Short-Term Loans to Others $ _____
- **6. *TOTAL CASH*** (lines 1 - 6) $ _____

PERSONAL ITEMS
- **7.** Principal Residence $ _____
- **8.** Furnishings & Electronics $ _____
- **9.** Jewelry $ _____
- **10.** Collectibles & Art $ _____
- **11.** Car(s) $ _____
- **12.** *TOTAL ITEMS* (lines 7 - 11) $ _____

INVESTMENTS
- **13.** Real Estate $ _____
- **14.** Businesses $ _____
- **15.** Retirement Plan(s) $ _____
- **16.** Certificates of Deposit $ _____
- **17.** Stocks & Bonds $ _____
- **18.** Insurance Cash Surrender Value $ _____
- **19.** Gold/Silver $ _____
- **20.** Other Investments: _____ $ _____
- **21.** *TOTAL INVESTMENTS* (lines 13 - 20) $ _____
- **22.** TOTAL ASSETS $ _____

LIABILITIES:
UNPAID BILLS
- **23.** Back Taxes $ _____
- **24.** Credit Card Debt $ _____
- **25.** Medical & Dental $ _____
- **26.** Other Bills: _____ $ _____

LOANS (principal only)
- **27.** Car(s) $ _____
- **28.** Personal Loans $ _____
- **29.** Insurance Policy Loans $ _____
- **30.** Education Loans $ _____
- **31.** Margin Account $ _____
- **32.** Other Loans: _____ $ _____

MORTGAGES OWED
- **33.** Home $ _____
- **34.** Investment & Rental Property $ _____
- **35.** Other Mortgages: _____ $ _____
- **36.** TOTAL LIABILITIES (lines 23 - 35) $ _____

NET WORTH (line 22 minus line 36) $ _____

Credit Card Payoff Calculator

Balance owed	$10,000	Months to payoff based on minimum payment	40
Interest rate	10.00%	Months to payoff based on proposed payment	22
Minimum monthly payment	$300	Total interest based on minimum payment	$1,764
Proposed monthly payment	$500	Total interest based on proposed payment	$985

Months to Payoff

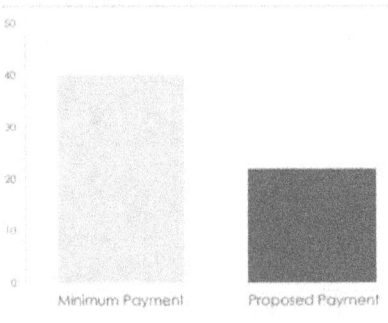

Total Interest

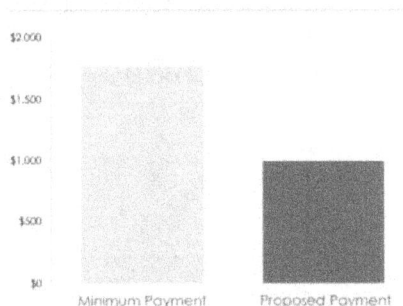

Emotion Frequencies

Hz	
700+	Enlightenment
600	Peace
540	Joy
500	Love
400	Reason
350	Acceptance
310	Willingness
250	Neutrality
200	Courage
175	Pride
150	Anger
125	Desire
100	Fear
75	Grief
50	Apathy
30	Guilt
20	Shame

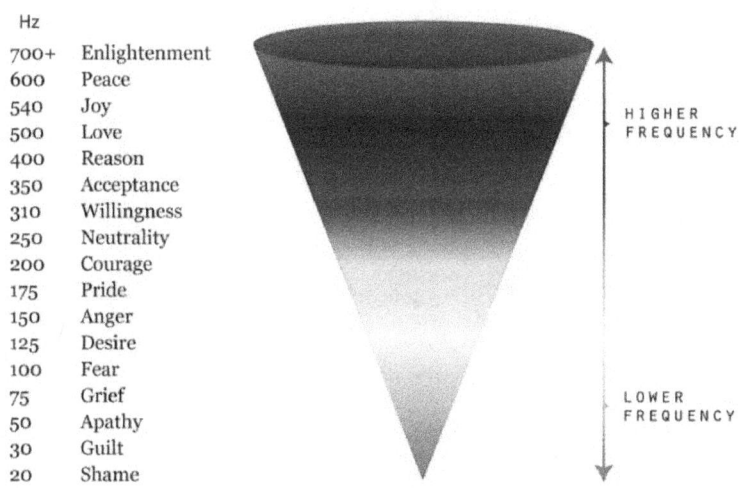

HIGHER FREQUENCY

LOWER FREQUENCY

Tax Efficiency Check-Up

Where is your money now?

Fill out the worksheet below, including your personal assets and business assets (where applicable) to evaluate what percentage of your wealth is in each bucket.

Tax Now (Taxes applied at current rates)		Tax Later (Taxes can usually be deferred; tax rates may vary in future)		Tax Free (Distributions income tax-free under certain conditions)	
Checking[1]	$	IRAs[3]	$	Roth IRAs[10]	$
Savings[4]	$	401(k), 403(b) Plans[6]	$	Municipal Bond Funds[11]	$
Mutual Funds[4,2]	$	Other Deferred Comp. Plans[6]	$	Whole Life Insurance cash value [12,14]	$
CDs[4]	$	Annuities[6,4] (fixed & variable)	$	Universal Life Insurance cash value [13,14]	$
Other	$	U.S. Govt. Savings Bonds[5]	$	Variable Life Insurance cash value [13,14]	$
Other	$	Business (privately held)[6]	$	529 College Savings Plans[15]	$
Other	$	Other	$	Coverdell Savings Plans[15]	$
Current Total:	$	Current Total:	$	Current Total:	$

Current Portfolio: $ _____

[1] Dividends and interest income may be taxed at the taxpayer's ordinary income tax rate in year earned
[2] Capital gains may be subject to short or long-term capital gains tax in year sold (including bonds sold before maturity)
[3] Withdrawals may be subject to ordinary income tax, and if made prior to age 59 1/2, may be subject to a 10% IRS penalty
[4] Surrender charges may apply
[5] Interest on U.S. government savings bonds are taxed as ordinary income in the year the bond is redeemed. However, an election can be made to report the taxable interest annually
[6] Income from sale/transfer (full or partial) may be taxed as capital gain or ordinary income depending on structure and source of funding specified in buy-sell transaction
10 Contributions to a Roth IRA may generally be withdrawn tax-free at any time. Earnings may generally be withdrawn tax-free if the account has been held for at least 5 years and the withdrawal is made after age 59 1/2. If the withdrawal is made before the 5-year period or age 59 1/2, income taxes and a 10% penalty tax may apply.
11 Interest income from municipal bond income may be categorized as a tax preference item tax under the Internal Revenue Code. This may trigger or increase AMT and may increase the amount of Social Security income that is subject to taxation.
12 Whole life policies: Owner accesses cash from the policy by a combination of surrendering paid-up additions (PUAs) and taking loans against the cash value. PUAs are attained by using dividends, which are not guaranteed, to purchase additional insurance and/or buy using additional premiums under an Option to Purchase Paid-up Additions rider to purchase additional insurance.
13 Universal life or variable universal life policies: Owner makes withdrawals of cash value and takes loans against cash value
14 Policy loans accrue interest at the current rate. Loans and withdrawals will decrease the policy cash value and death benefit by the amount outstanding.
15 Withdrawals not used for qualified higher education expenses may be subject to income taxes at the distributee's rate plus a 10% federal income tax penalty on the gains

THE FINANCE DOCTOR'S TIPS & TRICKS

Planning for Your Future

Key questions to consider

1. Are preservation of assets and financial independence important as you grow older and during retirement?

2. Do you have any personal insurance coverage in place that covers you or your spouse in the event of incapacity due to illness, accident, or simply the aging process?

3. Do you own any assets that produce income, such as real estate? If so, how many?

4. Have you already used (or do you plan to use) all of your lifetime exemption as part of an estate tax reduction strategy?

5. If you were to establish an irrevocable life insurance trust (ILIT), would you be interested in funding it in a way that could create income-tax free retirement income for you?

6. Do you have more than one child, heir, or beneficiary to whom you would like to leave assets?

7. Do you plan, or should you plan, to leave any assets or significant portions of your assets disproportionately among your heirs (business, stocks, farm, real estate, etc. to some but not all of your heirs)?

8. Do you have any grandchildren? Are you currently utilizing your annual gifting exclusion?

9. What techniques, if any, are you currently using to save for retirement? How do you plan to fund your retirement?

10. Do you care for someone with special needs??

11. If you were to pass away unexpectedly, could your family continue to pay bills and manage the household in your absence??

JHAYNE S. SANTUCCI

SCHEDULE A
(Form 1040 or 1040-SR)
(Rev. January 2020)
Department of the Treasury
Internal Revenue Service (99)

Itemized Deductions
► Go to *www.irs.gov/ScheduleA* for instructions and the latest information.
► Attach to Form 1040 or 1040-SR.
Caution: If you are claiming a net qualified disaster loss on Form 4684, see the instructions for line 16.

OMB No. 1545-0074

2019

Attachment Sequence No. **07**

Name(s) shown on Form 1040 or 1040-SR | Your social security number

Medical and Dental Expenses	**Caution:** Do not include expenses reimbursed or paid by others.		
	1 Medical and dental expenses (see instructions)	1	
	2 Enter amount from Form 1040 or 1040-SR, line 8b	2	
	3 Multiply line 2 by 7.5% (0.075)	3	
	4 Subtract line 3 from line 1. If line 3 is more than line 1, enter -0-		4
Taxes You Paid	5 State and local taxes.		
	a State and local income taxes or general sales taxes. You may include either income taxes or general sales taxes on line 5a, but not both. If you elect to include general sales taxes instead of income taxes, check this box ► ☐	5a	
	b State and local real estate taxes (see instructions)	5b	
	c State and local personal property taxes	5c	
	d Add lines 5a through 5c	5d	
	e Enter the smaller of line 5d or $10,000 ($5,000 if married filing separately)	5e	
	6 Other taxes. List type and amount ►	6	
	7 Add lines 5e and 6		7
Interest You Paid **Caution:** Your mortgage interest deduction may be limited (see instructions).	8 Home mortgage interest and points. If you didn't use all of your home mortgage loan(s) to buy, build, or improve your home, see instructions and check this box ► ☐		
	a Home mortgage interest and points reported to you on Form 1098. See instructions if limited	8a	
	b Home mortgage interest not reported to you on Form 1098. See instructions if limited. If paid to the person from whom you bought the home, see instructions and show that person's name, identifying no., and address. ►	8b	
	c Points not reported to you on Form 1098. See instructions for special rules	8c	
	d Mortgage insurance premiums (see instructions)	8d	
	e Add lines 8a through 8d	8e	
	9 Investment interest. Attach Form 4952 if required. See instructions	9	
	10 Add lines 8e and 9		10
Gifts to Charity **Caution:** If you made a gift and got a benefit for it, see instructions.	11 Gifts by cash or check. If you made any gift of $250 or more, see instructions	11	
	12 Other than by cash or check. If you made any gift of $250 or more, see instructions. You **must** attach Form 8283 if over $500.	12	
	13 Carryover from prior year	13	
	14 Add lines 11 through 13		14
Casualty and Theft Losses	15 Casualty and theft loss(es) from a federally declared disaster (other than net qualified disaster losses). Attach Form 4684 and enter the amount from line 18 of that form. See instructions		15
Other Itemized Deductions	16 Other—from list in instructions. List type and amount ►		16
Total Itemized Deductions	17 Add the amounts in the far right column for lines 4 through 16. Also, enter this amount on Form 1040 or 1040-SR, line 9		17
	18 If you elect to itemize deductions even though they are less than your standard deduction, check this box ► ☐		

For Paperwork Reduction Act Notice, see the Instructions for Forms 1040 and 1040-SR. Cat. No. 17145C Schedule A (Form 1040 or 1040-SR) 2019

REFERENCES

INTRODUCTION

Lusardi, A. (18 November 2015). *Financial Literacy Around the World: Insights from the S&P Global FinLit Survey*. Retrieved from https://gflec.org/initiatives/sp-global-finlit-survey/

Survey of the States. (2020). Retrieved from https://www.councilforeconed.org/wp-content/uploads/2020/02/2020-Survey-of-the-States.pdf

CHAPTER 1 – THE UNCOVERING

Emotional Quotient vs. Intelligence Quotient. (2020). Retrieved from "https://www.diffen.com/difference/EQ_vs_IQ#:~:text=IQ,-Diffen%20%E2%80%BA%20Social%20Sciences&text=Emotional%20Intelligence%2C%20or%20emotional%20quotient,%2C%20control%2C%20and%20express%20emotions.&text=IQ%2C%20or%20intelligence%20quotient%2C%20is,to%20assess%20an%20individual's%20intelligence.

Benedict, C. (2020). *Why do some smart people keep making the same dumb mistakes*. Retrieved from http://serenityonlinetherapy.com/iq-eq.htm#:~:text=skills%20in%20managing%20painful%20emotions,skills%20in%20managing%20painful%20emotions.&text=For%20our%20purposes%2C%20I%20define,problems%20through%20learning%20and%20reasoning.

Hawley, C. (28 October 2019). *Most Americans think they know more about money than they do*. Retrieved from https://www.kiplinger.com/article/retirement/t047-c032-s014-most-think-they-know-more-about-money-than-they-do.html

Kingsbury, K. (30 April 2019). *America is in a financial literacy crisis, and advisors can fix the problem.* Retrieved from https://www.cnbc.com/2019/04/30/the-us-is-in-a-financial-literacy-crisis-advisors-can-fix-the-problem.html

Conscious Power. (5 March 2018). *50 Universal Laws that affect reality | Law of Attraction*[Video]. YouTube. https://www.youtube.com/watchv=zEr-90Cpj_Q

Fearless Soul. (30 November 2017). *Follow your heart, your brain is stupid* [Video]. YouTube. https://iamfearlesssoul.com/follow-your-heart-your-brain-is-stupid/

CHAPTER 2 – THE CLEAR GOALS

Fry, R. (28 April 2020). *Millennials overtake Baby Boomers as America's largest generation.* Retrieved from https://www.pewresearch.org/topics/generations-and-age/

Underwood, C. (25 August 2020). *Generational Strategies for Engagements.* Retrieved from https://businessbrokeragepress.com/2020/08/industry-veterans-experts-updates-with-chuck-underwood-generational-strategies-for-engagements-webinar-8-25-2020/

All about the Silent generation. (2 December 2019). Retrieved from https://www.indeed.com/career-advice/career-development/generation-of-silents

Hoffower, H. (11 August 2019). *The Great Recession created a domino effect of financial struggles for Millennials.* Retrieved from https://www.businessinsider.com/how-the-great-recession-affected-millennials-2019-8

Generation Z News. (2020). Retrieved from

https://www.businessinsider.com/generation-z?IR=T&itm_source=businessinsider&itm_medium=ctgr_bii&itm_term=ctgr_hub&itm_content=millennials&itm_campaign=generation-z-2

Dimock, M. (17 January 2019). *Defining Generations: Where Millennials end and Generation Z begins.* Retrieved from https://www.pewresearch.org/fact-tank/2019/01/17/where-millennials-end-and-generation-z-begins/

How to build credit. (2020). Retrieved from https://www.experian.com/blogs/ask-experian/crediteducation/improvi-ng-credit/building-credit/

Kiyosaki, Robert. (May 2000). *Rich Dad Poor Dad.* New York, NY: Warner Books, Inc.

IRS Publications Online. (2020). Retrieved from https://www.irs.gov/publications

Kieso, D. & Weygandt, J. (1989). *Intermediate Accounting 6th Edition.* Hoboken, NJ: John Wiley & Sons, Inc.

Larson, K. & Pyle, W. (1988). *Fundamental Accounting Principles 11th Edition.* Homewood, Illinois: Irwin

Types of Retirement Plans. (2020). Retrieved from https://www.irs.gov/retirement-plans/plan-sponsor/types-of-retirement-plans

CHAPTER 3 – BASIC TAX & FINANCIAL CONCEPTS

CPE Depot. (4 August 2017). *Tax & Financial Planning for Retirement.*

Rama-Poccia, M. (13 November 2018). *What is Rate of Return and what is a good Rate of Return.* Retrieved from https://www.thestreet.com/personal-finance/education/what-is-rate-of-return-14779699

Tax deductions vs. Tax credits: What's the difference. (16 July 2020). Retrieved from https://www.creditkarma.com/tax/i/tax-deduction-and-tax-credit#:~:text=The%20big%20difference%20between%20tax,amount%20of%20taxes%20you%20owe.&text=Tax%20credits%20are%20always%20refundable%20or%20nonrefundable.

Frankel, M. (15 February 2020). *Your Guide to Tax Credit.* Retrieved from https://www.fool.com/taxes/2020/02/15/your-2020-guide-to-tax-credits.aspx

The three basic Tax types. (2020). Retrieved from https://taxfoundation.org/the-three-basic-tax-types/

Tarver, E. (23 August 2020). *Income Tax vs. Capital Gains Tax: What's the difference.* Retrieved from https://www.investopedia.com/ask/answers/052015/what-difference-between-income-tax-and-capital-gains-tax.asp

Choose a business structure. (2020). Retrieved from https://www.sba.gov/business-guide/launch-your-business/choose-business-structure#section-header-16

CHAPTER 4 – THE STRATEGIES

Macbride, E. (28 April 2020). *Backdoor Roth IRA.* Retrieved from https://www.investopedia.com/terms/b/backdoor-roth-ira.asp

Amount of Roth IRA contributions that you can make for 2020. (2020). Retrieved from https://www.irs.gov/retirement-plans/plan-participant-employee/amount-of-roth-ira-contributions-that-you-can-make-for-2020

Understanding Charitable Remainder Trusts. (2020). Retrieved from https://www.estateplanning.com/Understanding-Charitable-Remainder-Trusts/

What is Domestic Asset Protection Trust. (2020). Retrieved from https://www.assetprotectionplanners.com/asset-protection-trust/domestic/what-is/

Incomplete Non-Grantor Trusts: an effective tax planning strategy. (June 2020). Retrieved from https://www.bdo.com/insights/tax/private-client-services/incomplete-non-grantor-trusts-an-effective-tax-pla

Kennon, J. (9 September 2020). *How a Spendthrift Trust can protect your heirs from themselves.* Retrieved from https://www.thebalance.com/spendthrift-trust-can-protect-your-heirs-357479

Draper, L. (28 February 2020). *Spousal Lifetime Access Trust & the increased estate exemption.* Retrieved from https://regentatlantic.com/blog/spousal-lifetime-access-trust/

Hoffman, T., Havard, N. & Damm, E. (October 2016). *Spousal Lifetime Access Trusts: Not just for the rich and famous.* Retrieved from https://www.kmgslaw.com/knox-law-institute/publications/spousal-lifetime-access-trusts-slats-not-just-for-the-rich-and-famous

Why Captive Insurance may be right for you. (12 December 2018). Retrieved from https://www.morganstanley.com/articles/captive-insurance

Boyte-White, C. (17 July 2019). *Land Trust.* Retrieved from https://www.investopedia.com/terms/l/land-trust.asp

Soled, J. (1 August 2004). Cost Segregation applied. Retrieved from https://www.journalofaccountancy.com/issues/2004/aug/costsegregationapplied.html

How an Employee Stock Ownership Plan works. (24 August 2020). Retrieved from https:/www.nceo.org/articles/esop-employee-stock ownership-plan

Kenton, W. (28 February 2020). *Family Limited Partnership.* Retrieved from https://www.investopedia.com/terms/f/familylimitedpartnership.asp

What are Opportunity Zones and how do they work. (2020). Retrieved from https://www.taxpolicycenter.org/briefing-book/what-are-opportunity-zones-and-how-do-they-work

Weltman, B. (13 April 2017). *Qualified Small Business stock: What is it and how to use it.* Retrieved from https://www.sba.gov/blog/qualified-small-business-stock-what-it-how-use-it

Kenton, W. (2 January 2020). *Qualified Small Business Stock.* Retrieved from https://www.investopedia.com/terms/q/qsbs-qualified-small business-stock.asp#:~:text=A%20qualified%20small%20business%20is,as%20they%20meet%20certain%20criteria

Perez, W. (5 January 2020). *Home Improvement and Residential Energy Tax Credits.* Retrieved from https://www.thebalance.com/residential-energy-tax-credits-3193014

McGuire, D. (27 May 2020). *R&D tax credits and the coronavirus.* Retrieved from https://www.accountingtoday.com/opinion/r-d-tax-credits-and-the-coronavirus

CHAPTER 5 – THE GAP

Parker, T. (13 February 2020). *Savings Plans from College: 529 Plans vs. Roth IRAs.* Retrieved from https://www.investopedia.com/529-plan-vs-roth-ira-for-college-4771260

Compare Savings Options. (2020). Retrieved from https://www.savingforcollege.com/compare_savings_options/?assigned_to%5B%5D=0&assigned_to%5B%5D=1&hiddenField=vehicles&mode=Submit

CHAPTER 6 – THE EMPOWERMENT

Zaidi, A. (20 April 2014). *Think and Grow Rich – The 13 Principles from Napoleon Hill's Book*. Retrieved from https://mdi.com.pk/management/2014/04/think-grow-rich-13-principles-napoleon-hills-book/

CHAPTER 7 – THE EXECUTION

Rogers, T. (21 July 2020). *Want to become a Billionaire*. Retrieved from https://www.businessinsider.com/career-fields-industries-that-produce-most-billionaires-wealthx-report-2020-5#1-banking-and-finance-10

CHAPTER 8 – LIFE INSURANCE AND ANNUITIES

Kuepper, J. (12 January 2020). *Indexed Universal Life Insurance: Pros and Cons*. Retrieved from https://www.investopedia.com/articles/personal-finance/012416/pros-and-cons-indexed-universal-life-insurance.asp

Life Insurance and Annuities Fundamentals. (2015). Sandi Kruise Insurance Training

CHAPTER 9 – SECURITIES

Series 7 Top-off General Securities Representative Study Manual 42nd Edition. New York, NY: Securities Training Corporation

CHAPTER 10 – REAL ESTATE

Florida Real Estate Online Course. (March 2020), Orlando, FL: Climer Real Estate School

ABOUT THE AUTHOR

Jhayne S. Santucci is the Founder of Excelsure Consulting LLC whose mission is to provide expertise in business, tax, financial management, operational excellence, marketing, and technology. Excelsure provides C-Suite expertise as a business traverses from one million to the twenty-million-dollar revenue threshold.

Jhayne received her Bachelor of Science in Accounting in 1992 and started her career in Tax with the Big 4 CPA firms, PricewaterhouseCoopers LLP and Arthur Andersen LLP in Chicago. In 2001, she joined a startup healthcare service company while managing her tax preparation business. In 2006, she relocated to Central Florida with her young son to join a regional accounting firm that specialized in International Tax. In 2008, she started law school part-time and received her Juris doctorate three years later. In 2009, she joined the largest reseller and distributor of plastic resin, where she held various roles in the Tax, Corporate Accounting, Internal Audit, and Regulatory Compliance departments.

Jhayne's passion for helping others led her to recognize the need to promote financial education so she directed her focus from Tax and Accounting to Finance. In 2018, she received her Life & Health Insurance license. In 2019, she received her Series 7 license to become FINRA Registered Representative. In early 2020, she received her Real Estate license to be a Business Intermediary and assists clients with the acquisition process.

Jhayne supports various non-profit organizations such as the Asian American Heritage Council of Central Florida where she has served as a board member in the past 10 years. The organization's mission is to recognize and reward Asian American students for their academic excellence and exemplary community service and leadership. Jhayne is also a volunteer instructor at Score and teaches entrepreneurs how to build their financial plans.

Jhayne loves the beach and she makes sure that she travels every year to a place she has never been before.

Notes

Notes

Notes

Notes

Notes

Notes

Notes

Notes

Notes

Notes

Notes

www.ingramcontent.com/pod-product-compliance
Lightning Source LLC
LaVergne TN
LVHW051828080426
835512LV00018B/2774